D1311635

DISCARDED

PEABODY INSTITUTE LIBRARY
Danvers, Mass.

To my son Ben, who shared my love of science,
oceans and the Maine coast, and to future wildlife
stewards everywhere. — S.K.

To my wife Michelle Holmes, who got me
into the outdoors when we dated. We've never
come back indoors.— D.J.

Copyright © 2020 Stephen W. Kress and
Derrick Z. Jackson

All rights reserved. No part of this book
may be used or reproduced, stored in
a retrieval system, or transmitted by
any means — electronic, mechanical,
photocopying, recording or in any manner
whatsoever without written permission
from the publisher except in the case
of brief quotations embodied in critical
articles and reviews.

For further information, contact:
Tumblehome, Inc.
201 Newbury St, Suite 201
Boston, MA 02116
https://tumblehomebooks.org/

Library of Congress Control Number:
2020932831
ISBN 13: 978-1-943431-57-1
ISBN 10: 1-943431-57-4

Kress, Stephen W. and Jackson, Derrick Z.
The Puffin Plan / Stephen W. Kress and
Derrick Z. Jackson — 1st ed

Photos on the dedication page, copyright
page and page 180 by Derrick Jackson.

Design: Yu-Yi Ling

Printed in Taiwan
10 9 8 7 6 5 4 3 2 1

Copyright 2020, All rights reserved.

TUMBLEHOME

THE PUFFIN PLAN
RESTORING SEABIRDS TO EGG ROCK AND BEYOND

Stephen W. Kress & Derrick Z. Jackson

1.

LIZARD TAILS AND SPARK BIRDS

I grew up in Bexley, Ohio, a cozy suburb of Columbus. The mid-1950s, my childhood years, were a time when families let ten-year-old kids romp from house to house and disappear for hours alone at neighborhood parks. My greatest passion was exploring open spaces where I had a chance to catch a frog or toad.

My favorite park was Blacklick Woods, in part because it was just a twenty-minute drive from my suburban home. It contained old forests and undisturbed swamps. I felt different from most of the kids at school who seemed happy playing sports or hanging out. I felt most at home outdoors.

The moist swamp forest made Blacklick Woods rich with reptiles and amphibians, like wood frogs, spring peepers, and salamanders. Even though this was a park, I explored off the trails more than on them. Only poison ivy patches limited my exploring! Every weekend, I pestered my mom, Lina, to take me there.

She often dropped me off at Blacklick with a friend, Mac Albin, a bag lunch, and a dime in my pocket to call her from the pay phone when I was ready to come home. By the time she showed up, we were usually soaked and happily exhausted from our explorations. My mom was annoyed that we soaked the cloth car seats, but to her credit, she knew our swamp jaunts were important to us and put up with the mess.

I didn't realize it at the time, but I was so lucky to have a friend like Mac Albin living just down the street. Our mutual enthusiasm for nature made it all feel so normal to be outside. It didn't matter that other kids showed so little interest.

The park naturalists were our heroes. They saw that we shared their passion for nature. I found their "Junior Explorers" club more engaging than anything I was doing in school. After years of free ranging in the park woods, I wrangled a summer job cleaning cages in Blacklick's trailside museum. This led to end-of-summer gifts, including a four-foot-long rat snake and occasional raccoons or opossums that I brought home to my tolerant parents.

My 7th grade science fair project was my first science success, earning a red ribbon and membership in the Ohio Academy of Science. I used a trial and error approach to designing the homemade incubator — the beginning of a lifelong path of hands-on bird research. Photo by Herman Kress

My dad, Herman, owned a business that sold bags of all shapes and sizes. He was handy with wood working—a talent that was helpful for building cages for my ever-growing collection of frogs, snakes, and turtles. He even brought home box turtles he found on the road during his business trips to farms. All Mom asked was that I keep my "zoo" in the backyard or basement. Perhaps she took comfort from my Grandmother Anna's observation, "Don't worry — he'll outgrow it!"

While every creature, large or small, fascinated me, my favorite animal in Blacklick Woods was a lizard called the five-lined skink. To Mac and me, it was the greatest prize of all. Perhaps it was its rarity, or its speed at avoiding capture. Or perhaps it was the beautiful, neon-blue tails of young skinks.

The prize of prizes for Mac Albin and me was a sighting of a blue-tailed skink, the neon-tailed young of the five-lined skink. Photo by dwi putra stock via Shutterstock.

When we found one sunning on a stump, we would admire it for a moment, then pounce! But we rarely caught one. Skinks are food for a very long list of sharp-eyed birds, reptiles, and mammals, including herons, owls, hawks, jays, snakes, skunks, raccoons, and foxes. Only the fastest skinks survive. They also have a unique escape trick. When seized from behind by a predator, their tail may snap right off— leaving the twitching tail in the jaws of the predator... or in the hands of a frustrated boy!

Today we know that capturing wildlife, especially in parks, violates the ethics of respecting wildlife. A better way to "capture" wildlife is in a photograph. I hope children, whether in nature clubs, school trips, or scout programs, never lose the opportunity to explore in their backyards and nearby parks, because it will lead to many more adventures. Many years later, while doing college research, I learned that when children handle snakes gently and with respect, it helps to build positive feelings. Without such experiences, kids may fear snakes.

I credit my fourth-grade teacher at Montrose Elementary for sparking my interest in birds. One spring day, Mrs. Reed spotted a bird below her 2nd floor classroom window. She gathered the class around and asked, "Who can identify that brown bird pecking at the ground?" I ran to get the Golden Guide to Birds from the classroom shelf. When the robin-sized bird flew up, it flashed its white rump and yellow underwings. I found a perfect match with Yellow-shafted Flicker (now Northern Flicker). It was my first success at bird identification—my spark bird! After that, on many nights, my mom would find me, asleep, still clutching a Golden Guide.

My "spark bird" was a Northern Flicker, which I identified from the second floor of Montrose Elementary School in Columbus. Much later I learned that my birding guru, Roger Tory Peterson, also claimed the flicker as his spark bird. Photo by Helmer Nielsen.

As Mac and I entered our teens, we added birding to our list of animal adventures. At one Junior Explorer gathering, a naturalist mentioned that a local birder was willing to take kids birding with him, and he wondered if anyone in our club was interested. Of course, Mac and I leaped at this chance to explore further from home.

That birder was Irving (Irv) Kassoy. Born in Russia in 1904, Irv moved to the United States as a toddler. He was an original member of the Bronx County Bird Club, the legendary teen birding group whose members, including Roger Tory Peterson, later became ornithology leaders. Irv grew up to be a New York City jeweler and equipment supplier, but he was much more enthusiastic about birds than glittering diamonds. He was such an expert on barn owls that in 1936, the *New Yorker* magazine featured him as the "Owl Man." The article mentioned his thick eyeglasses and observed that he even looked like an owl.

By 1950, Irv sold his jewelry supply business and moved to Ohio. On weekdays, he was an upholsterer, covering furniture. On Saturdays, armed with binoculars and spotting scope, he became my birding superhero. He would arrive at my front door at dawn to pick up Mac and me as my parents slept. Off we went, looking for Rough-legged Hawks, Short-eared Owls, Barn Owls, Golden Plovers and any other birds that we found along the way. Despite his thick glasses, Irv was an amazing birder. He could spot birds miles away off the two-lane country roads that we prowled.

While other kids played sports, I tromped through corn stubble and grassy fields, counting short-eared owls. During the day, these owls roost together on the ground, so we would spread ourselves out in a long, straight line and walk across the field to flush the birds. On a good day, we would usually see 20 or more of these graceful birds.

Through Irv and other mentors, I also started going to birdwatching talks. On one momentous evening, Roger Tory Peterson was the featured speaker at an Audubon Wildlife Film series. Irv introduced us. I felt as if I was at the feet of God! I was so inspired being around these birders that, even though I was only sixteen, I wanted to attend an Audubon adult summer camp in 1963. The only problem was that one had to be 18 to attend. Undaunted, I wrote letters asking if they could use an enthusiastic helper.

I heard nothing from the camps in Maine and Wisconsin, but I was shaking with excitement when a letter arrived from Duryea (Dur) Morton, then-director of Audubon's camp in Greenwich, Connecticut. CONNECTICUT! For this Ohio nature boy, the letter could have just as well come from Mars. All I could think about was that Connecticut was far from Ohio and, even better, Greenwich was near the ocean. I could have walked on air with happiness. Later, I learned that Dur Morton hired me for exactly the same job he had when Audubon first hired him: student assistant dishwasher. He eventually rose to be National Audubon's vice president for education. He liked to joke, "All good men start as dishwashers."

Dur always gathered the student assistants together before the arrival of a new group of campers for a pep talk. At one meeting, he explained that since humans were the only species capable of destroying other species, we should be caretakers of life on Earth. This was the first time I had heard of the concept of stewardship. Suddenly, I realized I had been mistaken in catching and keeping wild animals, and I recalled those that had perished on my watch. For the first time, <u>I started thinking less about how to make animals part of *my* environment and more about taking care of *their* environment.</u>

Student assistants, even dishwashers, conducted nature projects of their own design. Mine focused on bullfrogs and their sounds. I noticed that every time an airplane flew over, the frogs sang. I was totally thrilled when Audubon Magazine expressed interest in my research and published it in 1964 as "Bullfrogs Sing Along with Jets." It was my first published writing, and I received a hundred dollars for it. I proudly framed the magazine's acceptance letter and hung it on my bedroom wall.

My first published research paper appeared in Audubon Magazine in 1965 when I was 19. It reported on my study of nocturnal frog calls at the Greenwich Audubon Center. Photo by Stephen Kress.

After four summers of working at Audubon camps in Greenwich and Wisconsin, Dur invited me to serve as a naturalist at a community nature center in St. Andrews, New Brunswick. Although I had hoped to work that summer at the Audubon Camp in Maine on Hog Island, I quickly accepted this position because it brought me back to the coast. My job was fun — exploring tidal pools with children and teaching bird biology to adults. But I lived for the weekends, when I got to explore more remote habitats. More good luck came my way when I met Mary Majka. She came to the nature center to take my birding class and stayed on as a volunteer.

I didn't know it at the time, but Mary was to become one of Canada's most famous naturalists, likened to Rachel Carson for drawing attention to birds and conservation. Like Irv Kassoy, she shared her passion and her wheels to take me on birding adventures. It was with Mary that I first saw puffins.

One weekend I drove with her and her family down to Cutler, Maine, just over the US border. Here we met Purcell Corbett, a Maine coast seaman who used only his watch and compass for navigation. He motored us 12 miles out to Machias Seal Island, an 18-acre jumble of boulders, surrounded by waves and seaweed. The lighthouse keeper, Jack Russell, offered birders overnight lodging in his home. Jack's wife, Rita, warmed us up with seafood chowder. Then Jack took us out onto the boulders.

This was my first visit to a seabird colony, and I was dazzled. In our first moments ashore, Arctic Terns attacked us with wild screams, pecked at our heads, and shot poop our way as we walked the boardwalk to the buildings. The attacks were for a good reason—parent birds were defending their fluffy chicks, hidden in nearby patches of vegetation.

My eyes could not have been wider at my first up-close view of puffins. They were everywhere, perching atop bird blinds, buildings, and high rocks. These otherworldly creatures, with their rainbow-colored beaks, bright eyes, and tuxedo-like black and white bodies, had me hooked forever! Jack proceeded to pull an adult puffin and a chick from their rocky burrows for a closer look.

At night, we searched under the lighthouse for another incredible sight: puffin fledglings working their way toward the sea. Puffin chicks, with no guidance from parents, leave their nests by night, when they feel the time is right, and scamper to the edge of the sea.

Normally, they head for light on the horizon. But on an island with a lighthouse, the chicks sometimes become confused and march to porches and doorsteps by mistake. Jack loved to tell the story of one very dark night when the fog was so thick, he could "slice it with a knife." Hearing a tapping at the lighthouse door, he opened the door cautiously to see who had knocked at such a late hour. At first, he saw nothing but the fog. Then he happened to glance down to see an eight-inch-tall puffin looking up at him.

I returned to St. Andrews for a second summer in 1968 and continued my weekend seabird adventures, always reaching further afield. Seabird islands were my passion.

My first puffin experiences were on Machias Seal Island, located on the Canadian/U.S. border. I stayed overnight in the lightkeeper's quarters and spent several days exploring the island during the summer of 1967. Now, Machias Seal Island supports about 5,000 pairs of puffins. Photo by Derrick Z. Jackson.

2.

WORDS THAT CHANGED MY LIFE

In 1969, Dur Morton wrote me with exciting news. A birdlife instructor position had opened at the Hog Island Audubon Camp, just off Maine's mid-coast. This was the first Audubon Camp, with an amazing history dating back to 1936. The invitation to work there was a dream come true and an opportunity I'd waited patiently for since finding out about it six years earlier when I first worked in Greenwich, CT.

My new position brought me closer to a new forest habitat and a gateway to more than fifty other islands, many of which were home to nesting seabirds. I accepted Dur's offer with a resounding and immediate "Yes!"

Hog Island, sweet with the smell of spruce and fir, is legendary in Audubon circles. The island underwent centuries of human activity. First came the Abenaki for the surrounding bounty of seafood, then European settlers who kept livestock that resulted in the island's name. In 1908, Mabel Todd, one of the editors of Emily Dickinson's poetry, became outraged when she discovered timber clearcutting on the island. Todd and her astronomer husband, David, made up their minds to purchase most of the island. Soon they established a rustic family camp in the spirit of Henry David Thoreau's retreat at Walden Pond, Massachusetts. Years later, the couple's daughter Millicent Todd Bingham gave the pristine island to the Audubon Society.

The Hog Island Audubon Camp brought me to Maine in 1969 as a bird life instructor. Here I discovered a book in the Camp library where I learned that puffins once nested on nearby islands until the late 1800s when hunters took too many for food and feathers.
Photo by Stephen Kress.

Once Audubon established its summer camp for teachers, a featured camp activity was boat trips to nearby seabird nesting islands. Popular field trips went to Western and Eastern Egg Rocks to see large colonies of Herring and Great Black-backed Gulls. These field trips remained the highlights of the Hog Island program when I arrived as birdlife instructor.

My curiosity about these islands led me to the camp library in the Hog Island Fish House, where I found a 1949 book titled *Maine Birds* by Ralph S. Palmer. The detailed

Hog Island Fish House.
Photo by Stephen Kress.

species-by-species accounts summarized data gathered by Arthur Norton, formerly curator of the Portland Society of Natural History. With still-vivid memories of visits to Machias Seal Island, I was excited to read the section on puffins.

I knew that puffins were nearly wiped out in Maine in the late 19th century by poachers who hunted seabirds for food and for feathers to decorate woman's hats. I learned that on Matinicus Rock, the last island in Maine where puffins clung to existence, only one pair of breeding puffins still survived in the early 1900s. At that point, conservationists started paying an armed warden to protect the birds.

As I read more, I discovered that puffins also once flourished on several other Maine islands. Palmer's most descriptive account was from Seal Island, 34 miles northeast of Hog Island. In a retelling of a 1923 report by Arthur Norton, Palmer wrote:

> *"This is the main breeding place of the puffin in Knox County. During the 1850s, parties visited in the evening and spread old herring nets over the rocks to capture the birds as they came forth in the morning. By 1886 only about 25 or 30 pairs remained. Their final extermination was probably affected the following year by the milliner's agents [collectors of feathers for woman's hats] who carried on a most destructive season's work at that place."*

What came next changed my life. Palmer noted that puffins once nested on Western Egg Rock and Eastern Egg Rock, just eight miles away from Hog Island.

> *"The puffin bred on these rocks prior to 1860 and ...there were 'considerable numbers' still on both rocks in the late 1870s. Hunting decimated the birds to only five or six pairs on Western Egg Rock by 1885 and over the next two years, the last of the birds disappeared from the place."*

When I read those words, "the puffin bred on these rocks," the Muscongus Bay of the late 1960s suddenly looked to me as if it was missing something. Realizing how different and diverse the bird community had been on the

Egg Rocks, I felt keenly that we were now seeing a much-depleted variety of birds. In my mind, the vibrant gull colonies that I was showing Audubon campers became a somber reminder that in spite of the work of conservationists who came before us, the puffins and terns were missing.

In the US, the late 19th century saw an immense slaughter of birds for the hat trade. Birds such as terns, herons, egrets, gulls, plovers and sandpipers were valued only for their market value. Those who hunted them saw them as feathers and meat rather than as amazing wildlife.

At first, it seemed that the odds of stopping the hunting were too slim to succeed. However, up in Boston, Harriet Hemenway, a matron descended from the wealth of New England's cotton mills, marshaled her outrage over the slaughter of herons. She held tea parties that resulted in the 1896 creation of the Massachusetts Audubon Society. In 1897, the group convinced Massachusetts lawmakers to pass a law banning the trade of wild bird feathers.

That ban stimulated an outburst of similar societies in many states and finally, federal action. In 1900, Congress passed a bill that banned killing birds and taking them over state lines.

In Maine, William Dutcher led the conservation movement. He set out to stop the slaughter of birds any way that he could. On one occasion, he tipped off federal agents to a stash of 26,000 gull skins in Baltimore. One of his highest priorities was to protect the seabirds of Matinicus

Rock, one of Maine's most important seabird homes. He hired the light keeper, James Hall, in the spring of 1900, giving Hall the distinction of being the first seabird protector in the country. Hall's reputation as "the finest

Matinicus Rock Light as it looked in about 1880 at the height of the seabird hunting, National Archive.

shot in these parts" helped him deter the feather hunters.

In the summer of 1901, Hall reported that the terns and guillemots had a good nesting year. He also mentioned that puffins "raised young during the season." Hall and his rifle may very well have saved the last pair of puffins in Maine.

By 1904, Maine had ten wardens, the most of any state. That helped inspire the federal government's establishment of the first national wildlife refuges. Dutcher went on to become the first president of what would become the National Audubon Society in 1905.

With protection, puffin numbers began to grow very slowly on Matinicus Rock. However, nearly seven decades later, when I first came to Maine in 1969, there were still only a few dozen pairs. These small numbers were very vulnerable to a storm, disease or hungry predator.

My new vision of a past rich in puffins and other seabirds led me to a deep sense of loss. I wondered if there just might be a way to bring the puffins back. The thought "What if?" began to haunt me. In my imagination, I saw flocks of puffins flying in, perching atop the boulders and popping into their rocky homes with beak loads of glistening fish. Obsessed by this vision, I began thinking how I would bring puffins home.

By coincidence, I was just starting graduate school at Cornell University in 1972 when an innovative effort began to bring back the Peregrine Falcon to the eastern United States. The noble peregrine, fastest of all animals, had disappeared from eastern states, victims of widespread use of the insecticide DDT. But a dedicated group of falconers were determined to help falcons and other birds of prey such as eagles and ospreys recover after DDT was banned in 1972.

Peregrine Falcon restoration was just starting at Cornell in 1972 when I began my graduate studies. Photo by Harry Collins via Shutterstock.

The peregrine project encouraged me to stick with my hope for a puffin comeback and to come up with a plan. I told Dur Morton and other Audubon officials about my idea, and they encouraged me to come up with a plan.

I read everything I could find on the topic.

I learned that puffin parents raise their chick underground, bringing it whole finger-sized fish that they drop
at the chick's feet. Chicks eat the fish on their own until
they reach fledging age and head out to sea. Years later, the
puffins return to nest near where they hatched. That gave
me the idea that if I moved puffin chicks soon after they
hatched and raised chicks by hand at a different location,
they might return to nest at the release site rather than to
where their parents nested.

With encouragement from my Audubon mentors, I began writing to other seabird researchers seeking their opin-
ions about restoring a puffin colony. One of my first letters
went to Ralph S. Palmer, author of the 1949 book that first
inspired my thinking. I assumed that he would lend me a
sympathetic ear because of his retellings of puffin destruc-
tion in his book *Maine Birds*. I was thrilled when I received
an envelope from nearby Tenants Harbor, Maine where
Palmer lived. I eagerly opened the letter, but my enthusiasm was dashed when I read his response. He told me my
idea was a waste of time. He said anyone who wanted to see
puffins should go to Iceland where they could see millions.

I was disappointed that Palmer missed the point of my
still untested puffin comeback. People had caused puffins
to disappear from Maine islands, and they had not returned
on their own to any of their historic nesting places. Since
people caused them to disappear, I felt that people should
also try to bring them back, much as the Cornell researchers

were trying to help the peregrines. I reasoned that since the small puffin colony on Matinicus Rock was slowly increasing, ocean conditions and food supplies were still good for puffins along the Maine coast.

I also hoped that if I could learn how to bring back puffins, the methods I developed could help other rare and endangered seabirds. I had read about the tragic extinction of the puffin's distant cousin, the Great Auk. When people slaughtered these large, flightless birds, no one stepped forward to save them from extinction. The last Great Auk died in 1844 at the hands of a museum collector in Iceland. Reading about this loss made me more committed than ever to try to help puffins and other threatened birds.

Great Auk
by John Gerrard Keulemans.

Fortunately, puffins survived the era of seabird hunting at remote locations in Canada. When I began thinking about bringing puffins back to Egg Rock, there were about 500,000 pairs in Canada, with 300,000 of them residing on three islands near Saint John's, Newfoundland. That may sound like a lot of birds, but it was only a fraction of the number that used to live there. Puffins were also abundant on many islands off Nova Scotia in the early 19th century, but by 1922, they were largely gone from most of their southern range.

As I thought about Egg Rock, I wondered why gulls were thriving, while the puffins had never came back on their own. After all, both gulls and puffins were protected from hunters. Why the difference?

Eventually, I realized that gulls were benefiting from an abundance of food from fishing waste and nearby open land-fills. In contrast, fish-eating birds such as puffins, murres, razorbills and gannets couldn't eat discarded human food. These species had little chance to start new colonies as long as the predatory gulls dominated all of the possible nesting islands.

Puffins did not naturally return to their historic nesting islands in Maine in part because of a resurgence of predatory gulls that benefitted from fishing waste and scraps at landfills. Photo by Stephen Kress.

One reason nobody was acting to bring back puffins and other lost species was the prevailing idea that it was best to "let nature take its course." Even as raptor researchers were actively working to bring back the peregrine by moving eggs and chicks and releasing captive-reared young, most seabird biologists felt that it was wrong to "play God." They assumed that a new "balance of nature" would eventually set in. Some species would prove able to live along humans, and others would be lost. This vision of the future was bad news for puffins and most other species that neither directly benefited from humans nor attracted dedicated interest groups such as hunters or falconers.

The more I thought about it, the more I was convinced that the idea of letting "nature take its course" was wrong. After all, humans had caused puffins and other seabirds to disappear in the first place. It made clear sense to me that other humans should work to bring the birds back to places where they once lived. I did not know it at the time, but this view of bringing birds back to nesting islands would become known as seabird restoration.

Razorbills, murres and puffins have increased at Matinicus Rock in recent years with protection from predators. Photo by Stephen Kress.

Seeking more advice, I contacted William Holland Drury Jr., one of New England's leading seabird experts. At the time, he held the position of research director at the Massachusetts Audubon Society. I sent him a letter and draft proposal in August 1971 sketching out my plan for a puffin comeback. I wondered if I would even hear from him and was wary after the Palmer put down. After all, I was an unknown upstart with few credentials. I was thrilled when I received not only a quick response but an invitation for a visit.

I found the esteemed Dr. Drury tucked away in a back office surrounded by stacks of papers and books. Tall, lanky, and mostly bald, he welcomed me warmly. We had an upbeat talk about Maine seabird islands, as he had once conducted gull censuses on the Egg Rock islands in Muscongus Bay and he even knew they were once puffin nesting islands.

Drury was among the first to understand that human influence affected nature everywhere. In short, if humans did not "play God" by favoring rare species, the species that thrive around humans, such as gulls, would be the ultimate winners. He thought my idea of bringing puffins back to the Egg Rocks was part of such a vision.

On my new mentor's advice, I wrote to David N. Nettleship of the Canadian Wildlife Service. As Canada's top expert on Atlantic puffins, Nettleship approved permits to visit sanctuaries. He would be the one to assess the idea of restoring a puffin colony by moving puffin chicks to former nesting islands.

With a hopeful cover letter, I sent Nettleship a draft proposal for collecting puffin chicks at Machias Seal Island, chicks that I hoped to rear and release at Eastern Egg Rock. In a courteous reply, Nettleship noted that I put a lot of thought and careful planning into my proposal. Nevertheless, he believed Maine's location at the southernmost end of the puffin's North American range made the state merely a "peripheral" breeding ground. He thought that at the least bit of environmental or climate stress, the birds would retreat toward Canada. In short, he denied my request.

David Nettleship's reply stung me as much as the rebuff from Ralph Palmer.

Sunrise at Matinicus Rock with terns. Photo by Stephen Kress.

3.
SETBACKS AND UNKNOWNS

The regional director of the Canadian Wildlife Service seconded David Nettleship's refusal to let me collect puffin chicks from Machias Seal Island. His letter said my experiment would "irresponsibly deplete the colony and thus was contrary to their objectives."

I delivered this sobering news to Bill Drury. He responded by writing Nettleship.

Drury pressed the possibility that my project could actually help Canada's puffins. He explained that because there were just two colonies existing at the time along the Maine and New Brunswick coasts—Machias Seal and Matinicus Rock—both still recovering from 19th century hunting, it made sense for the two countries to collaborate. Together they could create "seed colonies" at historic puffin nesting islands. New colonies would help to bolster the population and bring puffins back to a more expansive range. Drury argued that more colonies would reduce risk from local threats. With all of the puffins at just two islands, it was like having "all of the eggs in just two baskets" should disaster strike such as predators, oil spills and disease.

Dr. Drury on Little Duck Island holding a young gull with students from College of the Atlantic. Photo provided by John Anderson.

Drury begged Nettleship "not to close the door on a young man's immature plans."

Though David Nettleship remained skeptical of a "rosy future" for puffins in Maine, he agreed to meet with me in person in Ottawa in August of 1972.

In the months before our meeting, I decided to practice chick rearing with Black Guillemots, a puffin cousin that already nested at Egg Rock. This plan seemed to make sense, because chicks of both species live in rock crevices, eat whole fish and head to sea (fledge) on their own without guidance from parents.

Guillemots were also hunted to the brink of statewide extinction. By 1903, once-huge colonies of guillemots plummeted to just 75 pairs on only 14 of Maine's 4,613 islands. Unlike puffins, with protection from hunting, they rebounded on their own. By the early 1970s, Drury estimated there were 3,400 pairs of guillemots nesting in Maine,

Because Black Guillemots and puffins are related to each other, I thought I could learn some things from guillemots that would help me raise puffin chicks. Photo by Melissa Groo.

and they had reclaimed most of their former nesting islands.

I obtained permits to collect six guillemot chicks from nearby Franklin Island where they nested in the rubble of an old lighthouse keeper's home. I started out rearing them in cardboard boxes lined with newspaper on the porch of a Hog Island cabin.

From the beginning, the guillemot chicks were hard to raise. They usually eat ribbon-shaped rock eels that I could sometimes find under rocks in the intertidal zone, but they were far too scarce, so I tried feeding strips of frozen fish.

Flying black Guillemot (top) and Black Guillemot with red rock eel (bottom). Photos by Melissa Groo.

This seemed like a good idea, but it was the beginning of a humbling cascade of disaster. Oil dribbled out of the fish and stained the bird's breasts. Then the chicks soiled their feathers by sitting in their poop.

When the first guillemot reached fledging age and sported its full set of juvenile feathers, I released it into the ocean, but as it swam away, it sank lower and lower, until only its head was above water. Something was dreadfully wrong. It should have sat high and dry, shedding water, but instead the feathers soaked up water. Then I realized that this sad little bird lacked waterproofing. Its feathers were too dirty, and now the water was pulling the chick down. I tried to retrieve it, but it had paddled off into deep water and the fog soon engulfed it forever.

I tried to test the waterproofing of the remaining five chicks by floating them in an antique claw-footed bathtub. All had lost their waterproofing. There was no remedy. I released them in their less-than-ideal condition, saddened that this first step of the project was so discouraging. I wondered what I could learn from this setback.

Like puffins, Black Guillemots nest in rock crevices where they speckled eggs on flat rocks and colorful shells. I was humbled by the simplicity of a guillemot nest, yet it was so difficult to replicate a similar nest in captivity. Photo by Stephen Kress.

The failure made me go back to Franklin Island to take a harder look at guillemot chicks in natural nests. Here I found fledging-age chicks with immaculate feathers in their

3-day-old Black Guillemot Chick in hand. Like puffin chicks, Black Guillemot chicks are fluffy and bright eyed. They can walk around in their underground home the day after they hatch. Rock eels are their favorite meal. Photo by Stephen Kress.

simple, clean rock crevices. I learned a critical lesson. Keep it simple and natural. Newspapers and cardboard were far from the natural light and climate of a rock burrow where chicks received whole fish. This was also one of my first lessons to remain humble. Guillemot parents were much better than I was at selecting rearing places and providing the right kind of foods for their chicks.

When I went to Ottawa, I met a far different Nettleship than what came across in his rejection letter. He was not all that much older than I was, having only recently finished his graduate studies with Newfoundland puffins. He was also deeply enthusiastic about seabirds and conservation, and we could easily discuss our common passion of seabird conservation. He shared his own research with puffins, in which he had successfully kept chicks in captivity for growth studies. Together, we began talking about how it might be possible to transplant chicks as a pilot study in the following summer. He invited me to incorporate his suggestions into a new proposal. Based on his encouragement, I promptly set out to write a new proposal.

Months slipped by without me hearing anything. Finally, after five months of checking my mailbox for some written word (this was before the days of email and text messages), I held my breath and gave Nettleship a call to inquire about the proposal. I braced for another rejection, but the news was just the opposite. He told me that my proposal was approved to collect six puffin chicks!

Much to my surprise, the chicks would not come from Machias Seal Island. Instead, I could collect them on Great Island in Newfoundland. I could have walked on water at this news. Not only did I have a green light, but also I would be visiting the largest puffin colony in North America—home to about 160,000 pairs of puffins. After hanging up, I let out a huge whoop of excitement. With news of the permission, I received another boost—my first successful grant application. It was an award of $2,700 from Audubon to help with the pilot study.

The thrill was soon tempered with the reality of the challenges ahead. While Machias Seal was 34 miles away from the Hog Island camp, Great Island was a thousand miles away. This created all kinds of unanswered questions

I had not anticipated, such as how would I safely transport the chicks, and what permits would I need?

One thing was certain. Because I was still teaching at Hog Island, I knew that I would need an assistant to help me take care of the chicks. My first choice was Kathy Blanchard. She served as a student assistant at Hog Island in the summer of 1972, and I knew she was diligent and meticulous with a keen interest in birds. Her dad was from Newfoundland, which gave her a special connection and interest in the project. I asked her to be my first assistant to help rear the puffin chicks.

Now that the project was real, it hit me how fragile my dream was. I was setting off on largely uncharted waters. There were so many questions. How would I keep these six chicks alive for hundreds of miles of bumpy roads from Newfoundland to Maine? How and what would I feed them? How would I keep them clean while bringing them from Newfoundland to Maine? How old should the chicks be when I collected them? What to feed them? What kind of rearing burrows should I use? Would they even survive the long trip to Maine?

Then it dawned on me. No one had ever started a puffin colony before. I would need to discover answers as I went, learn from my mistakes and keep my eye on the goal of bringing puffins back to Egg Rock—and I would only have six precious chicks in this first year.

The only relevant experience I had was with Black Guillemots, and that had been a clear disaster. I could only find two previous examples of anyone even trying to start a seabird colony. These were attempts to start colonies of Laysan Albatross and Short-tailed Shearwaters by translocating chicks. Both projects failed.

I worried that if my plan also failed, that would likely confirm people's belief that restoring seabird colonies was an exercise in foolishness and futility.

I felt the weight of the conservation world on my shoulders. I had to prove the doubters wrong.

Black Guillemot swimming away. Photo by Stephen Kress.

4.

PUFFIN PARADISE

There was an awakening in the early 1970s about taking care of our planet. The first Earth Day happened in 1970, and President Nixon signed the Endangered Species Act and other important conservation laws. Against this backdrop, my trip to Newfoundland to collect six puffin chicks was a tiny event, but to me it was a huge moment.

Kathy Blanchard joined me for the trip. Her great-grandfather was a fisherman, seal hunter, and captain of a schooner that had transported people, goods, and coal for the lighthouses between Nova Scotia, and southwest Newfoundland. Her father and grandfather were also from Newfoundland and shared her passion for nature. She dreamed of a conservation career, but her high school guidance counselor told her that there were not many jobs for a girl who loved the environment. She ignored that advice and applied for a job at the Audubon camp. In her camp application, she wrote, "I want this more than anything in my life."

Now we were on a quest that I wanted more than anything in my life. David Nettleship agreed to two trips in the summer of 1973. The first was to scout for collection locations and to take temperature measurements of the microclimate in burrows. I reasoned we would want to create similar conditions in chick-rearing burrows in Maine. We would collect puffin chicks on the second trip in July.

Our first trip was in mid-June. John Reddick, whose family had fished for cod and salmon in Witless Bay for decades, took us out to Great Island. We saw puffins nearly as soon as we left the dock, and the numbers increased as we approached the island. We passed some plump birds sitting on the water holding fish called capelin in their beaks. Some were so fat, they could barely fly.

Great Island was a dramatic sight, easily in view from the mainland. Icebergs that had floated down from Greenland surrounded it. At a distance, it seemed covered in snow and ice, but I could see with binoculars that the cliffs were covered in guano (seabird poop) and there were vast swarms of birds coming and going. For someone who had only seen a small colony of puffins previously, this was all beyond my wildest imagination.

As we approached the towering cliffs of the island, we were wide-eyed at the close-up views of Black-legged Kittiwakes wheeling overhead as they screamed their namesake call: "kitti-wake-kitti-wake." Then our focus changed. We were approaching the island and needed to pay close attention to land safely. We motored as close as we could into a small cove and then transferred from John's motorboat to his bright orange wooden dory.

Great Island kittywake cliff.
Photo by Stephen Kress.

This was a special landing boat that we had towed out to the island for the final approach. In the cove, we found a yellow rope hanging overhead between two cliffs. One of John's brothers rowed the dory and another snagged the rope with a boat hook. Clearly, they had done this before for other researchers, but I was so dazzled by the sight

Orange dory at Great Island.
Photo by Stephen Kress.

and sounds of thousands of birds that I could barely hear the boatman's voice: "Jump—jump now!"

There was no time to hesitate as the dory rose on a surging swell up against a huge slippery rock. I jumped on command and saw the dory drop quickly with Kathy and the boatman below. Then it rose again and she leapt from the dory to the landing rock. Immediately, the dory slipped away into the fog, and we were alone in this vast paradise of puffins, murres, kittiwakes and other seabirds.

First landing on Great Island. Photo by Kathleen Blanchard.

Puffin burrows were everywhere: on the grassy slopes, among the tangled roots of the spruce forest, and among boulders at the base of the steep cliffs. In flat regions the grass was lush and green, benefitting from the guano of puffins and the million pairs of Leach's Storm-petrels that honeycomb the soil. In some places, the tunneling and guano from puffins had killed

I was amazed by the size of the fish puffins were carrying. Parent puffins were feeding their chicks capelin, a northern fish that was the perfect size and shape for their chick.
Photo by Jef Combdon via Shutterstock.

With permission from the Canadian Wildlife Service, we landed on Great Island, Newfoundland to collect ten-day old puffin chicks. Here, Kevin Bell and Mike Haramis reach into puffin burrows to find chicks the right age.
Photo by Stephen Kress.

the vegetation, exposing the soil to erosion. Nearly everywhere, alert puffins stood at burrow entrances, intently watching our approach.

Even though there were about 160,000 puffin pairs nesting here, we soon learned that obtaining large numbers of chicks would not be easy. We began to explore the different habitats and discovered that burrows on the flat part of the island were far too deep to reach chicks. Likewise, burrows under tree roots were also too deep and twisted to reach chicks. Alas, we could only reach chicks in burrows on the steep cliffs, a dangerous undertaking at best.

On the cliffs where we could reach puffin chicks, we also had to contend with slippery grass, guano and Great Black-backed Gulls. This is the largest species of gull in the world, with a nearly six-foot wingspan. The gulls were not happy to have us on the cliffs near their chicks. To drive us away, they swooped and screamed, missing direct hits by inches while we clung to the slippery slopes. A missed step here or a direct hit by a gull would knock us off the steep cliff into the sea below.

Only slightly flustered by the gulls and dizzying heights, we continued with our exploration and managed to take temperatures within many puffin burrows. Surprisingly, we found the burrows consistently cool at any time of day or

Great Black-backed Gull on nest.
Photo by Stephen Kress.

night, always about 55°F. This steady temperature became our target when building new burrows in Maine.

A month after this scouting trip, we returned to collect the six puffin chicks for the pilot study. We were very fortunate that Peggy Morton introduced me to a neighbor named Bob Noyce. He was the co-inventor of the integrated circuit microchip and the cofounder of Intel, which today remains a global giant in the computer processing industry. Noyce liked my innovative plan and offered to fly Kathy and me to Newfoundland and back in his private plane. This slashed days of bumpy road travel that would have stressed the chicks.

Kathleen Blanchard (left) Bob Noyce (green jacket) and co-pilot collecting puffins at Great Island. Thousands of puffins dot the fog covered island. Photo by Stephen Kress.

The flight eastward along the Maine coast and then over the Maine and New Brunswick forests was stunning— so many islands, so many lakes. For the first time, I had a sense of what a migrating bird might see over this magnificent coast.

John Reddick again took us out to Great Island, and we collected our six chicks. I placed them in a special carrying case made of juice cans and plywood with a swinging door to provide access. Front and back of the case were covered with burlap to give the chicks ample ventilation. We spread silicone caulk on the bottom of each can, and sprinkled sand into the tacky surface to provide a good grip for the chicks' feet. No detail was too small for our precious passengers.

We also collected food to bring back to Maine for the chicks. We wanted them to have familiar tasting capelin, so we scooped up a bag full from a nearby beach where the fish came to lay eggs. To the casual onlooker, capelin is just

David Nettleship and Evelyn Weinstein with carrying cases on Great Island, Newfoundland. Photo by Stephen Kress.

another small silver fish, but it is the critical forage fish—the vital bridge between zooplankton, whales, seals, cod, and most seabirds, including puffins.

I kept the chicks by my side on the plane while Bob whisked us back to Maine on Sunday, July 15. At last, Project Puffin was really beginning.

Once back to Hog Island, we placed three chicks in hand-made rock burrows on the shore of Hog Island. We had cobbled these together from small chunks of granite and cement before going to Newfoundland. I hoped that replicating natural burrows would be better than rearing chicks in artificial boxes and cages indoors. We were not sure about these outdoor burrows, however, so for safety, we placed the other three puffins in wooden boxes in the air-conditioned porch of the Binnacle, my Hog Island cabin.

After we fed the last of the capelin to the chicks, I thought it would be best to provide freshly captured fish from the shoreline of Hog Island. One hopeful idea for catching fish was to

We searched for puffin chicks that were about ten days old. At that age they could stay warm without brooding from parents. We hoped that about a month of life on Egg Rock would give the chicks a memory of their new home. Photo by Stephen Kress.

build a trap modeled after a herring weir. Kathy and eager campers from Hog Island went to great lengths to build the trap in long cove. Though the idea was promising, no one had experience building weirs and we were all surprised by the power of the tide and weight of seaweed that soon collapsed our fish trap. We ended up buying frozen smelt and vitamins to feed the chicks.

The Hog Island campers were beside themselves with curiosity, so I brought one of the fluffy black chicks in its box outside so that some fifty adult campers could see it. The chick huddled in the corner, emitting a whiny call as a long line of campers cued up and waited their turn to peek in the box, each whispering good wishes to the fluffy chick like so many wise men who had come to see the baby Jesus.

However, our excitement was short-lived. Just a few days after the transplant, one of our three puffins from the rock burrows was missing! At first, we suspected our own shoddy handiwork. We discovered a crack in the burrow large enough for the chick to escape. We immediately applied cement to the crack and checked every nearby crevice to find the breakout chick. Alas, we found nothing.

Sober with regret over losing one of our precious puffin chicks, we decided to entomb the remaining two chicks in their burrows by cementing hardware cloth over the burrow entrances. We left just a tiny opening through which we could slip in their food. The next morning we were shocked to find the hardware cloth pulled back partly from one of the remaining burrows. A close examination showed a few telltale raccoon hairs on the wire.

We brought the remaining two puffin chicks indoors until we could double our security by repairing the wire mesh over the burrow entrances and building a large chicken-wire cage over the rock burrows. We also set a large live trap on the rocks for the suspected raccoon and baited it with cat food. We caught nothing.

Though we were completely committed to the care of the puffin chicks, we also continued raising several guillemot chicks to see if we could improve on our disastrous waterproofing results of the year before. We decided to test our reinforced rock burrows with one of the guillemots and two of the remaining puffin chicks.

We kept the other guillemots in a large chicken-wire pen adjacent to our rock burrows. The pen took days to build as we pounded posts into the mud and strung chicken wire more than 30 feet from the low water to dry land. We

In 1973, I visited both Western and Eastern Egg Rock, inspecting them for locations to rear and release puffin chicks. Both islands were historic puffin nesting islands and I wanted to see which one had the best nesting habitat. I landed at Western Egg Rock with David Morton (left), Kathy Blanchard (right) and Grace Bommarito. We were soaked from our landing, but managed to set up camp and explore the island. After visiting both islands, I settled on Eastern Egg Rock because it had more boulders under which puffins might someday nest. Photo by Grace Bommarito.

were proud of our engineering, as the pen would give the birds high and low water-swimming opportunities with the tidal changes. Our hope was that this would give the birds plenty of ocean water to help them clean their feathers and stimulate preening.

But our optimism instantly vanished. Kathy checked the guillemot chicks at dawn and was crushed by her discovery. A raccoon had breached our maximum-security protection and killed all the guillemots in the pen. She held the pathetic remains—a couple of detached guillemot legs. It was the saddest day of the summer.

By early August, the puffin chicks were almost old enough to fledge, and we knew we had to get them off Hog Island before a raccoon caught them. We visited Eastern and Western Egg Rocks, the two nearby historic puffin nesting islands, to see which would be best for releasing the chicks. Puffins had not nested on these islands since the late 1800s, but it was clear that Eastern Egg Rock was the best site, because the large boulders reminded me of the puffin habitat at Machias Seal Island.

Some of the boulders on Eastern Egg were of glacial origin, dropped thousands of years ago when ice fields retreated from Maine. But most were more recent, snapped from the underlying bedrock and then rolled into place during extreme storms. The result was a natural apartment complex with many opportunities for nesting under the jumbled boulders. Although the highest part of Egg Rock is just 17 feet above the high tide mark, most of the boulders were high enough to provide dry nesting habitat for puffins.

Several days before we brought the chicks to the island, Kathy and I hauled bags of cement to Eastern Egg Rock and gathered small granite chunks to build five release burrows on its southwest shore. Then, on August 17, 1973, we put the remaining five chicks in a box and took them to Eastern Egg Rock—likely the first puffins to be on the island in about 100 years.

First five puffin fledgers in box at Eastern Egg Rock, Aug. 1973.
Photo by Stephen Kress.

I banded each chick with a green-coiled plastic band on one leg and a metal USFWS band on the other. We placed each chick in its own rock crevice burrow and secured wire doors over the entrances to give the chicks a chance to settle in until dark. Then we would remove the covers and hope the chicks would make their way to the sea. Still nervous about predators, we knew the puffins were safe from raccoons, but now we feared that gulls might swoop in and carry off the chicks. So, we waited until midnight, when most of the gulls would be asleep, to open the burrow entrances.

Kathy's journal notes document the excitement of seeing the fledglings make their way to the water. Most of the chicks walked, climbed over boulders and eventually scrambled into the surf.

But one of the pufflings made a more dramatic departure. On August 19, Kathy described in her journal how she watched puffin number three leave its burrow and move steadily toward the sea. Sometimes it tumbled out of sight, and then scrambled back to the surface. Finally, it crawled up a tall rock overlooking the sea, where it stood for about five minutes. It seemed as if it was trying to get the nerve to fly for the first time. Several times it leaned forward with rapid beating wings and finally pushed itself into the air. Then it flew above the crest of the waves and disappeared into the darkness. Kathy wrote that she was "thrilled and honored to witness this special moment!"

We had banded the chicks with the hope that we would someday see them again, but I knew these chicks were likely a sacrifice for science, because most young birds never survive to breeding age. It would take many more chicks to have a chance at starting a colony. Our primary goal in this first year had been to prove that we could translocate chicks from Newfoundland to Maine and rear them to fledging age. The puffin chicks looked cleaner than our guillemots, but we could only hope that they had better waterproofing. There was no way to know for sure.

At summer's end, I reported to Nettleship the successful fledging of the chicks and my greater appreciation for the stamina of puffins. I focused on the positive, emphasizing that we demonstrated that we could transport chicks safely from Newfoundland and raise them to fledging age at Eastern Egg Rock. I just needed more time and more puffins. Remembering Bill Drury's wisdom, I asked Nettleship for his advice on future steps. He was clearly interested now in the outcome of this unusual project. About two weeks later, he wrote back giving his support for more chicks next summer.

I could have walked on air!

These first five birds were our victory—they represented an enormous amount of effort, trial and error, and no small amount of just dumb luck. The five puffins were pioneers, each one a little miracle. It was amazing that they were now out at sea completely on their own. While the eventual outcome of the project was unknown, I had tasted the thrill of our first success and was ready to take on the many challenges ahead.

Egg Rock storm. Photo by Rose Borzik.

Egg Rock Campsite, 1974. Photo by Duryea Morton.

5.
LIVING WITH
SEABIRDS

W e were confident that with enough care and vigilance, we could rear a small number of puffin chicks to fledging age. That was the message from the five chicks released in 1973. A small number was one thing, but now we had permission to move 58 chicks in 1974.

For continued success, we would need to make some big changes to our methods. Some things were perfectly clear. It was obvious that we should attempt to rear the chicks in as natural a setting as possible, and that meant outdoor burrows. But Hog Island was a bad place to rear puffin chicks. Even one raccoon was too much to manage.

Besides, we wanted the chicks to learn that Eastern Egg Rock was home, not Hog Island. We would need to raise the chicks on Egg Rock—but that would require people living with the puffins all summer to feed and protect them. It also meant dealing with gulls.

Herring and Great Black-backed Gulls and almost all other birds received protection from hunting with passage of the Migratory Bird Treaty Act of 1918. The large numbers of gulls that I saw on Maine islands in the early 1970s was proof that gulls clearly benefitted. Yet other seabirds remained scarce. The smaller seabirds could not return to their former nesting islands in part because these islands had become huge gull colonies. It would be suicide to nest among the gulls.

While most gulls are scavengers, some are excellent predators, and the puffins did not want to take a chance of

Large numbers of gulls can dominate nesting habitat.
Photo by Stephen Kress.

becoming dinner for a gull. Local garbage dumps and fishing waste made life very easy for Herring and Great Black-backed Gulls. Puffins didn't have a chance of returning to the Maine coast with so many gulls crowded onto these former nesting islands.

I concluded that to bring puffins back, we had to chase off the gulls.

To move the puffin comeback plan forward, I organized a team to go out to Eastern Egg Rock in June of 1974 to prepare for the puffin chicks that would arrive in mid-July. Kathy and two new research assistants, Nina Davis and Roger Eberhardt, joined me for the trip. Fittingly, we went out to the island aboard the Puffin III, the Hog Island Camp boat, piled high with camping gear, lumber for building a tent platform and an odd assortment of materials to build puffin burrows. We were joined by Frank Gramlich, Maine's federal supervisor of wildlife services. He came armed with the avicide *Starlicide*, a poison developed to control European starlings.

Gramlich was an expert on the tricky subject of when to kill animals and when to aid their recovery. In the 1960s, he field-tested chemical control of urban pigeons in Bangor. In the 1970s, he spearheaded federal coyote control to benefit farmers in the West.

But he opposed bounties for coyotes in Maine as unnecessary. He also launched a program to bring Bald Eagle eggs from Minnesota to Maine eagles who laid infertile eggs due to the pesticide, DDT. Gramlich chose *Starlicide* to reduce the number of gulls. A month before this trip, he visited Egg Rock by himself to start the control. He placed small bread sandwiches with a margarine/*Starlicide* mixture in the gull nests. At the time, there were only about 100 gulls on the island.

He recalled his first trip. "The gulls were taking the bait just fine. I figured that would clean them out." But now it was June and Gramlich exclaimed, "Look at them! There must be four hundred around the island now!"

This time, he came armed with 600 *Starlicide* sandwiches. As he laid them down, he also crushed about 400 gull eggs. As he did that, he discovered the red feet and feathers of a Black Guillemot, likely devoured by a Great Black-backed Gull. In yet more evidence of what gulls can do, our presence scared scores of Double-crested Cormorants off their nests. The gulls quickly plunged on the cormorant eggs and made a quick meal of them. Watching the gulls raid the cormorant nests, Gramlich soberly reflected, "This control program is no solution to the gull problem. It's only a stopgap." We all knew that we would need to find a better way to manage gulls.

While Gramlich went about his business, we started building artificial burrows. I hoped that chimney tiles would serve this purpose. These were rectangular, two-foot-long, ten-inch square tubes designed to fit into chimneys that I obtained from a nearby lumber store. The tiles reminded me of hollow rocks, and I hoped they would work as a burrow substitute. We brought sixty onto the island and lugged them to the southwest shore. We strapped three tiles together inside wooden frames and positioned them among the granite boulders. We secured wooden boards to the back of the tiles to create a dark space within and fashioned wire mesh doors over the front of the tiles to keep chicks from escaping before they were ready to fledge. We even built cement ramps so the chicks could easily exit the burrows and make their way to the sea. Nothing was too good for our precious puffin chicks.

We hoped the ceramic burrows would be perfect new homes. But when we checked the temperature inside, we discovered they were like little ovens. On sunny days, they measured 92 degrees by noontime! This was forty degrees higher than the 50-degree temperature of a Newfoundland soil burrow. To help solve this new problem, we began

The first team to spend the summer living on Egg Rock. Left to right: Roger Eberhardt, Nina Davis, Steve Kress, Kathy Blanchard. ponder the fate of our 1974 puffin chicks in tile burrows.
Photo by Duryea Morton.

cutting thick layers of sod from nearby grassy areas to cover the tiles. We hoped this would provide insulation and lower the temperature inside the burrows. As a backup plan, Nina started digging a few hand-dug earthen burrows as a possible alternative.

While they prepared Egg Rock for the puffin home coming, Kathy, Roger and I headed to Newfoundland in mid-July. Our pilot was again the generous Bob Noyce. We met Bob at a small airport in Wiscasset, a half-hour drive from Bremen and Hog Island.

The next day, John Reddick once more boated us out to Great Island. Nettleship provided a map to show where we could collect chicks and more details about suggested ages and wing lengths for determining age. We were to take chicks between 10 and 18 days old, believing chicks of this age were old enough to maintain their own body temperature. We hoped they were too young to remember their native Newfoundland. Since no one had translocated puffin chicks before, this was a huge gamble.

Puffins look cuddly, but reaching into a burrow is not something to take lightly. Parent puffins have a sharp beak with a raptor-like tip. They are not shy about planting their crusher beak around a finger or sinking the tip into the loose skin between a researcher's fingers and hanging on with great determination.

To collect our 58 chicks, we reached into more than six hundred burrows. Most burrows were too deep to reach the contents. We could reach the contents of others, but they usually contained eggs, chicks that were too young or chicks that were too old. By pulling chicks and measuring their wing length, we eventually reached our goal. We carefully packed the chicks in cases made of juice cans, one chick to a can. We carried the chicks to the landing cove, said farewell to Great Island and began the long trip home.

Our first stop was in Bangor, Maine, where the chicks were examined by veterinarians who checked them for poultry disease. Agriculture Dept. inspectors probed the bottoms of each chick with a cotton swab to check for poultry disease, and four chicks were taken to a zoo to remain in quarantine. The remaining chicks were cleared for the final leg of the trip to Egg Rock.

We left the Audubon dock at dusk, but it was dark by the time we arrived at Egg Rock. We would have had a difficult time landing, except that Nina and Leslie Morton stood by the shore, swinging glowing Coleman lanterns. Like a lighthouse with twin lights, we could see Egg Rock at a distance. As we approached, we saw the greeters' faces reflected in the light. It was a haunting, almost Halloween-like scene. Audubon's head boatman, Joe Johansen, rowed us ashore in his long wooden dory.

Fortunately, the tide was high and the wind was calm. So many things were in our favor. The longest day of the year for me was almost over, but we still needed to tuck the chicks into their new homes. By lantern light, we carried the cases across the island and transferred each chick into its new home, along with half a small fish called a smelt.

We finished at midnight, seventeen and a half hours after collecting the first chick on Great Island. Exhausted and exhilarated, we toasted the chicks' arrival with a bottle of Newfoundland Screech (rum) that we brought along for this special occasion. My vision of bringing puffins back to Egg Rock had taken a giant step forward. We had earned our rest, yet we knew the really hard work was still ahead.

The next morning, I resumed my role as Hog Island birdlife instructor, but my mind was 98 percent still at Egg Rock, where Kathy and Roger were elated to find that all of the chicks had survived the night and were eating well. For their first full meal, the team fed each chick four smelt halves, each cut with a tapered end so the chicks could easily swallow. It was the chicks' first Egg Rock breakfast, the first of three daily meals.

After each meal, Kathy and Roger collected and buried leftover fish to reduce the risk that we would attract gulls. They also recorded the number of leftover fish as an alert that a chick had lost its appetite.

Nina Davis delivers a handful of thawed fish to puffin chicks in tile burrows. Photo by Duryea Morton.

Because the fish were frozen and may have lost nutrients, we followed the advice of the curator of ornithology at the Bronx Zoo, Joe Bell, to stuff some of the fish with vitamin B_1, vitamin E, and a multiple maintenance vitamin. The vitamin fish were carefully placed on top of the other fish, so the chick would most likely eat the vitamins.

The days that followed the transplant were unusually warm, and our temperature readings showed that our fear of overheating burrows was coming true—even with sod roofs. We piled more sod on top of the burrows to keep them as cool as possible. Thunderstorms then cooled the air with lashing wind, and rain swept over the island, collecting in puddles that produced vast mosquito swarms. The mosquitoes were everywhere, but the puffin chicks ate through it all.

After about a week, we took our first chick measurements. They were growing fine, but we noticed things that gave us concern. Some burrows let in too much light, leaving the chicks without a hiding place in a dark corner. To solve

The tile burrows developed problems immediately. Trying to keep ahead of the cascade of challenges, we adapted as we went to each new problem. Overheating led to burying the tiles under roofs of thick sod; bright interiors led to new covers with semi-circular entrances. Accumulated poop in the burrows led to regular cleaning. Photo by Duryea Morton.

this glitch, I cut plywood door covers with a round hole to mimic a soil burrow entrance and thus reduce the light. But now we worried that this would also reduce air circulation. We also learned that some of the fish were too large for the chicks to swallow, so we fed more of the tail pieces and carefully trimmed each piece with scissors to make it easier to swallow.

We also realized that our makeshift burrows lacked a key feature of natural puffin burrows—a sharp turn to the left or right into a dark nest cavity. Curved burrows also provided a toilet area, which reduced the chicks' risk of stepping in poop on the floor of the burrow. This feature of the burrow helped to keep feathers clean and waterproofed for life at sea. When we started finding poop accumulating on the floor of the burrow, we scraped it out with a spoon and removed it daily. While doing this, I kept thinking how amazing it was that puffin parents could create a natural burrow with all of the right features that didn't require cleaning and how natural foods were just the right shape and provided nutrition without adding vitamins!

As the chicks approached fledging age, we modified the entrances with "nocturnal activity indicators" (soda straws set on nails) that tumbled off when chicks exited. Photo by Duryea Morton.

Despite our best efforts to modify the burrows, we discovered that five pufflings were wet around the head and back, and their breasts and bellies were badly stained with poop. Nina and Roger thought the wetness was due to condensation from hot bird breath on the ceramic walls of the burrow and from the excess poop in the back end of the burrows where the chicks spent most of their time. They estimated that two-thirds of the burrows were filthy or wet.

As if that were not enough, they also found ticks on the faces of two chicks.

We launched into an extreme cleaning of the tile burrows. It was an ugly task. We scraped the crud out of the corners and pulled it out with a board. Wiping with a damp cloth left the burrows relatively clean, but it was traumatic for the birds, which were placed in a box while the cleaning was under way.

Desperate to reduce the accumulation of poop and stressful handling, we reduced meal size by half. We were clearly flying blind, but somehow the chicks lived. In the midst of this, Bob Noyce showed up in his sailboat. Roger and Nina pulled out a chick to show Bob how much it had grown in a week and a half.

But soon after Bob left the island, we discovered another tick in the nostrils of a chick. We worried now that we were importing not just puffins but puffin parasites that might infest future nestlings. We had inspected all of the chicks before their arrival from Newfoundland to ward against such a problem and had removed many ticks while on Great Island. Then a couple of days later, we noticed a puffin infested with feather lice. A veterinarian in nearby Damariscotta, provided us a powder to remove the lice. This puffin parenting was a huge job! Despite the setbacks and worries, the chicks continued to have good appetites and readily ate on their own.

As fledging time approached in late summer, we knew that the chicks would soon start stepping out of their burrows at night to exercise their wings. Still worried about gulls snatching the chicks, we built chicken-wire exercise enclosures around the burrows. But the chicks became so energetic that our makeshift exercise pens became injury risks, so we removed the pens and left the chicks to determine when and how they would fledge. By this time, most were banded with a metal Fish and Wildlife Service band on one leg and a blue plastic coil on the other leg.

We worried mostly about the chicks with soiled breast feathers. Wondering if the chicks had lost their water proofing, we put one of the most soiled birds in a large cooler filled with salt water. Happily, it seemed to shed water. But we didn't want to take more chances and moved the most soiled birds into newly-dug, 18-inch-deep soil burrows. Digging burrows turned out to be hazardous work as it sent up clouds of ragweed pollen. Roger was so allergic to the pollen that he had to stay out of the tall vegetation, leaving most of the digging to Nina. She also began to swell up in response to

After the tragic water proofing failure of our hand-reared Black Guillemots, we floated the first puffin chicks in a large cooler to see if their feathers shed water. Photo by Duryea Morton.

breathing too much pollen, but soldiered onward and finished the digging, dosed with medicine that left her groggy.

As we scrambled to move chicks into better burrows, a subtropical storm bore down on us. Roger checked the burrows at 4:30 AM and discovered that our first chick had fledged—into the storm! Then at 8 AM, he discovered that one of the chicks in an earthen burrow had escaped by digging around its hardware cloth door. The bird had dug so hard into the burrow's foundation that the structure caved in a few hours later. That would have been fine except that the chick left before we could band it.

As the chicks fledged, our project began attracting distinguished guests. Two of them were Carl W. Buchheister and his wife, Harriet. The couple held an iconic place in the Audubon Society. Carl was Hog Island's first director in 1936 and worked his way up to President of the society by 1959. In the early years of the camp, Carl and Harriet would take staff on boat excursions to Matinicus Rock, where puffins were slowly making a comeback. He championed the protection of puffins and other Matinicus Rock seabirds and visited the island for 45 years, spending summers among the seabirds from the late 1930s to 1957. For these reasons, he was especially thrilled to be on a seabird island again—especially one with puffins.

We showed the Buchheisters a puffling, which Carl photographed with much delight. I was personally indebted to Carl, for it was his stories about journeys to Matinicus Rock that had made me dream of one day living among seabirds. This moment was certainly a full-circle visit, with Carl and Harriet my guests on Eastern Egg Rock and me showing them a puffin.

The boost from that visit kept us focused as the challenges kept coming. In mid-August, one of our ceramic burrows hit 90 degrees. We tried to convince ourselves that a chick must be sitting on the thermometer, but the reality was that our chick homes were becoming ovens. We kept piling on more sod.

Then we noticed that gull numbers were increasing just as the chicks were reaching fledging age. We feared that gulls would snatch the puffins as they tried to make their way to the sea, so we alerted Frank Gramlich, and he quickly arranged for a return visit. This time he carried twenty pounds of *Starlicide*-poisoned fish and another bag of fish without poison.

He and Kathy walked around the island to spread the fish. Gramlich scattered poisoned fish while Kathy dropped fish without poison with the hope that the large amount of fish would attract all the gulls and they would eat all of the fish. To our surprise, the gulls had a different plan. They only ate the non-poisoned fish! Apparently, even though Gramlich had not visited the island since spring, the gulls remembered him and avoided the poisoned bait.

It would have been remarkable enough that gulls remembered their kin dying from the *Starlicide* sandwiches, but to associate a new bait dropped by Gramlich as poison was truly astonishing. It seemed that the gulls saw Gramlich as a mortal enemy, while viewing Kathy as a "friend." I was humbled by this and gained new respect for the intelligence of gulls. Other researchers have since demonstrated that crows can recognize individual people by their facial features. Apparently gulls can do the same. This taught us to never underestimate the intelligence of gulls.

By mid-August puffin chicks began moving to the sea in a big way. On August 16th, Roger witnessed seven puffin chicks make their way to the water. Now, with all of the burrows open, the chicks bounced from burrow to burrow. A couple of times, two chicks were seen in the same burrow. On August 17th, as hummingbirds buzzed the island on their way south, two more puffin chicks left. On August 18th, four more chicks took to the Atlantic despite sustained winds of 25 miles per hour. By dawn of August 21st, we were down to our last three pufflings, and by dawn of the 24th, the last had paddled off to the sea.

For the first time in months of nonstop trial and error, we could breathe a sigh of relief and dare to talk of *success*. All the chicks fledged! None of the Newfoundland transplants died in transit or in our oven-like burrows, nor were they decimated by ticks, lice or gulls. Despite the imperfections of their human "parents," all the pufflings fledged with normal body weights.

There were definitely some concerns that the birds with soiled feathers would have trouble with their waterproofing, but the vast majority appeared fine. In achieving a 100-percent fledge rate, we learned an enormous amount about rearing (and how NOT to rear) puffin chicks. We were encouraged by their natural vigor and adaptability to our experiments with food, vitamins, and burrows.

On September 3rd, I wrote David Nettleship to report that all 54 chicks fledged from Egg Rock. I hoped he would see that the chicks were in good hands and that we could continue with even more puffins next summer. I was filled with hope that we had taken a huge step toward our ultimate goal of reviving this lost puffin colony, even though there were still so many unanswered questions.

6.

PATIENCE, PERSISTENCE AND A PUFFIN!

N ow the real work began. The next seven years were a head-first journey into a swirling sea of mystery, frustration, hope, and most of all patience. To pursue my puffin vision, I needed to stay a step ahead of being written off as a fool.

We started the 1975 season with great news. David Nettleship was so impressed with our ability to raise puffin chicks to fledging age, he expanded the number we could take from Great Island to 100. To handle the larger puffin numbers, I recruited some special talent to help me rear the puffin chicks. The three research assistants for 1975 were

Tom French, Kevin Bell and Mike Haramis.

Tom hailed from the Atlanta suburbs. As a youth he was an avid birdwatcher and Boy Scout. Kevin was the son of Joe Bell, curator of birds at the Bronx Zoo. While most New York City children woke up to the honking of car horns and the screeching of subway brakes, Kevin's day began with birds squawking, lions roaring, and primates grunting. At age ten he did chores for his dad, everything from cleaning dung to reaching into the incubator to turn over eggs and look over the hatchlings at night.

Haramis was a fellow grad student at Cornell who was on his way to becoming an expert on the nesting habits of Wood Ducks and Canvasback Ducks. He was also an experienced duck hunter, a useful skill for gull control. This was necessary, because by 1975 the gulls were now wise to Gramlich and looked the other way when he offered *Starlicide*.

The opportunity to increase the number of puffin chicks to 100 made us realize that we could no longer micro-manage the temperature in blazing ceramic burrows. Moving toward more natural burrows, we abandoned the ceramic tile design in favor of digging burrows into Egg Rock sod. Our new plan was to dig 100 sod burrows in the deepest pockets of soil on Egg Rock.

We found the deep soil by pounding a metal rod into the sod, hoping to find two feet or more of soil before we hit rock below. Then we tried to imitate a natural burrow by twisting our digging trowel sharply to the left or right to create "L" shape burrows. This would give the chicks an opportunity to have a toilet area and a hiding place from predators. We pulled up all the ragweed sprouts that we could, knowing that they could quickly grow to clog the entrances and cripple our crew with allergies. Once again, I was in awe about how puffins dig perfect burrows, just with their clawed, webbed feet and with a beak that serves as an ax and shovel.

These new burrows seemed to work well with our 94 chicks (six went to a zoo for quarantine to guard against poultry diseases). Happily, the burrows stayed cool and we rejoiced that they were much more like natural burrows, making cleaning unnecessary. One wrinkle was that after just a few days, the chicks recognized when we were coming with meals. Many started to chirp with anticipation for their next feeding. This was disturbing because we wanted the chicks to stay as wild as possible. I wondered if tame chicks would venture too close to humans when they returned as adults. I pictured them landing on boats begging for a meal from a surprised lobsterman! In response, we set a no-talking rule when we were near the chicks.

Raising chicks in soil burrows was going so well that the crew could enjoy the nature around our tiny seven-acre island. Minke whales surfaced 100 yards off shore. Kestrels soared overhead, nighthawks cut the air at dusk, seals basked at low tide, and a large shark circled the island, showing off a huge dorsal fin. We also found time to forage at low tide for intertidal foods like periwinkles (invasive snails), which we steamed and sprinkled on our salads. We occasionally caught dogfish shark for dinner and, on a few occasions, a storm blew a loaded lobster trap up onto our rocks.

One chick died, but by the end of July, the 93 surviving chicks were healthy and about ready to fledge. Then, just when everything was going perfectly, heavy rains in early August flooded two-dozen burrows, soaking and soiling the chicks. Alas, the dense granite under the soggy soil backed water up into the burrows.

We were shocked to find that some burrows were completely full of water. It was a miracle that chicks didn't drown in a watery grave. On discovering this mess, we retrieved the soaked chicks and brought them back to the tent where we dried them off with towels. While Mike and Kevin hustled to build more burrows, we used our tent as a play pen for the rescued chicks until their new burrows were ready.

By mid-August, we knew the chicks were approaching fledging age, so we sat on the rocks at night hoping to hear the clinking of their metal bands on the rocks as they made their way to the sea. With luck, we sometimes saw them, their bright white breasts reflecting moonlight. I couldn't help but wonder how the little chicks knew what to do.

They were clearly running on instincts that would help them know where to go and how to find food (just like wild reared chicks). They would need a lot of luck to make it at sea — to avoid predators and find their way to places with ample food. We had done everything possible to send them on their way in good condition, but we could only hope that they were making a map to find their way home. The novelty of our experiment left us hoping for the best. Patience was our best friend.

Soon the last of the chicks headed to sea. In a thrilling moment that made us feel we did everything as right as we could, a bird-watching boat trip from Hog Island Audubon Camp spotted one of our chicks on the open water, sitting high and dry as we hoped. It was the first proof that our chicks were indeed waterproof.

David Nettleship informed me that we would receive permission for another 100 chicks in 1976. That was also the year we finally saw progress with gull control. Between Gramlich's grim work and the accurate eye of Tom with his rifle, the gull colony declined to about 200 birds. This was mainly because the gulls had learned to fear Tom and his rifle. We liked this approach of 'educating' the gulls rather than needing to kill them.

The flooding of our 1975 burrows inspired us to think about a new burrow design. While hand-dug burrows were certainly a step in the direction of natural burrows, there were good reasons that the original population of Egg Rock puffins nested in rock crevices rather than soil. Now we could see why. The soil was too shallow and vulnerable to flooding.

Like many inventors, we kept stumbling on improvements, learning from our mistakes. We abandoned the hand-dug burrow and switched to a burrow completely built of sod above ground. It was elegantly simple. We first created L- shaped sod foundations and then placed a large section of sod for a roof. The challenge was moving this heavy sod across the island from our "sod mines."

Research Assistant Mike Zaccardi (Zac) developed a primitive tool that we dubbed a "sod car." This consisted of a pair of two-by-fours separated by a three-by-four-foot plywood board. It proved key to moving mountains of heavy turf. Some of the larger sod blocks measured three feet by four feet across and about a foot thick. Moving chunks of sod this size required two strong backs to carry each load. In this way, we built a hundred sod burrows in just a couple of weeks.

In 1975 we abandoned the tile burrow idea and started building burrows from sod. These "puffin condos" were designed to have an L-shaped burrow entrance and a dark nest chamber. Because they were built above ground, they were safe from poor drainage issues. Patterned after natural soil burrows, the new design provided cooler and cleaner living space for the puffin chicks. Photo by Stephen Kress.

Left: Egg Rock puffin burrows in construction. First floor in foreground before sod roof (background). Right: Completed sod burrows with "street numbers" and dowel "activity indicators." Photos by Stephen Kress.

Amid our creativity, the first major doubts crept in. Puffins don't actually breed until around five years old, but they often start returning to the island of their hatching when they are two years old. There was no sign of our five birds from 1973 or the 54 from 1974 or 93 birds moved in 1975.

Tom Fleischner, a 1976 puffineer, provides a meal to the puffin chicks.
Photo by Stephen Kress.

The National Audubon Society maintained its faith in Project Puffin in the summer of 1976 by naming Eastern Egg Rock the Allan D. Cruickshank Wildlife Sanctuary. That meant a lot to me since Cruickshank, who had died a couple years earlier, was a friend of my mentor Irv Kassoy and a birding legend at Hog Island. My birding hero Roger Tory Peterson came to the dedication with Carl Buchheister, my inspiration for seabird conservation.

The good luck continued. The new sod burrows were proving a great success. We celebrated cool burrow temperatures, no flooding, and clean puffin breasts as 98 of our 100 chicks grew to the brink of fledging in mid-August. Then came our biggest challenge yet: Hurricane Belle.

The storm hit Long Island, New York as a Category 1 storm, causing $100 million in damage. When it got to New England, its winds were still hitting seventy miles per hour.

Although I encouraged Tom and Robert Wesley (a botanist friend from Ithaca) to leave the island, they wanted to ride out the storm in case the puffins needed to be evacuated from their burrows to higher ground. As it turned out, we had done a better job than we knew with our new burrows. Despite spray pounding the island and an ocean that looked like an agitator washing machine, the chicks remained snug and dry. None of the chicks were wet!

As if a bonus for their dedication, a loaded lobster trap washed up with dinner for the puffin keepers. Soon after, all 98 chicks fledged.

Nettleship approved another hundred chicks in 1977. But I worried that we should start seeing some returns by now. If we didn't see them soon, it would be difficult to make the case for more puffins and to make convincing statements that the project was on course for success.

I began trying to think like a puffin. I wondered whether, if puffins were coming back, they would come ashore without seeing other puffins on the island. For colonial seabirds like puffins, the absence of their kind is a signal for danger. Typically, young puffins come back to visit the colony where they hatched during mid-summer of their second or third year, hang out with adults for several weeks, and then head back to sea. Without any adult puffins already on the island, would returning puffins come ashore? I wondered what I could do to encourage puffins to land on the island, if any were in the area?

I thought of waterfowl hunters who use decoys to lure ducks and geese into hunting range, as did shorebird market hunters in the late 1800s. I also remembered a National Geographic article that showed how puffin hunters in Iceland will prop up dead puffins to serve as decoys to attract other puffins so hunters can snag circling birds with long nets. I wondered, could I turn a bird killing tool into a bird restoration tool?

Kathy Blanchard, who was now working for the Quebec Labrador Foundation (QLF), told me she thought the idea would interest Donal C. O'Brien. He was a Wall Street lawyer and a world-champion decoy carver whom she knew from her work with QLF. O'Brien was immediately enthusiastic about our decoy plan. Along with Connecticut carver Ken Gleason, he carved puffin decoys in standing and floating postures. These were then replicated on a wood lathe.

Children in an Ithaca elementary school helped to paint the decoys.

In June of 1977, Joe Johansen, assistant boatman John Ryan, Kathy, and I headed out to Egg Rock with 44 floating and standing design puffin decoys. I followed Joe in the Lunda, our research boat, as we planned to stay several days on the island. We connected the floating decoys in strings of 4 and used a brick to anchor each string of decoys to the ocean floor. I could easily imagine a puffin winging in to find company among the decoys. We were about to set more decoys when Joe noticed the wind increasing and a huge rain squall approaching. Always thinking of our safety, he rowed us ashore as the sky turned very dark. The remaining decoys would need to stay in the Lunda on the mooring for another day.

We got to shore just in time. The squall hit the island with such huge force that it flipped the Lunda on her mooring like a toy boat, dumping the rest of the decoys into the sea. Some of the floating decoys came ashore in a tangled mess, but most disappeared into the open ocean. Fortunately, I put our contact information on the bottom of the floating decoys. Days later, we started hearing about them washing up along the coast of southern Maine, some as far as seventy miles from Egg Rock. One was found 130 miles to the south in Provincetown, Massachusetts. The person who found it wrote to let us know where it was—and to inform us he planned on keeping it as a doorstop!

We called the Coast Guard to help us flip the Lunda back right-side-up. While waiting for our rescuers, Kathy and I turned our attention to putting out the twelve remaining standing decoys. We cemented these on high outcrops and boulders. Almost as soon as we set up the decoys, Great Black-backed Gulls attacked, knocking the decoys over with their feet before the cement could even dry. After just one attack, the gulls learned that the decoys were fakes and settled down to take a nap near the decoys. This moment of avian comedy was another example of the intelligence of the gulls. By end of the day, the Coast Guard managed to flip over the Lunda, and Kathy and I were towed back to Hog Island.

Just a few days after we put up the decoys, I was delivering supplies for Tom and Dave Enstrom, a young birder who later became an ornithologist at the University of Illinois specializing in blackbirds. As Tom rowed out to greet me, I spotted a quick-winged bird flying low over the water. I couldn't believe it.

It was an adult puffin!

Tom and I watched the puffin make several passes. After circling the landing area several times, it landed in the water between us, just a few feet away. As it bobbed in the water, I studied it carefully with my binoculars. It had one ridge on the orange part of its bill, indicating it was just two or three years old. Older birds would have two or more ridges.

The puffin was amazingly tame and just sat on the water looking at us, despite our screaming in disbelief. On the

Puffin on deep blue sea, Eastern Egg Rock.. Photo by Stephen Kress.

water's surface, the bird stood up and exercised its wings, then dipped its head in the water. It flew around Egg Rock several more times before plunging into the ocean near us again.

I was beyond joy—but then my heart almost stopped. A Great Black-backed Gull noticed the lone, vulnerable puffin. It dove at the little bird several times, but the puffin slipped under the water to safety each time. The frustrated gull finally called off the assault.

Then, in classic Hollywood script, it was just me and the puffin. It stopped diving and calmly stared at me.

Could it possibly recognize me for bringing it from Canada? Could I get close enough to see if it was banded? I edged the Lunda closer hoping not to spook it. "Yes!" It was banded!

I zoomed back to Hog Island and ran up the hill. Joe was mowing the lawn and Kathy was indoors. I shouted, "A puffin has returned!" Kathy and I sped back to Egg Rock with my camera. More than an hour had passed, but the puffin was still in the water, curiously picking at the bobbing handle of a red lobster buoy.

For the next 10 days, either Tom, Dave or local lobstermen reported puffins in the waters around Egg Rock.

We were so excited, we put up 10 more standing decoys. A week later, Dave was making pancakes for breakfast when he saw two puffins fly by the campsite. Both landed among the decoys, where he could see that one of the puffins wore a white leg band! This was proof that it was banded as a Newfoundland chick in 1975 at Egg Rock. The other puffin was unbanded.

The puffins cautiously approached the decoys, bowed, picked at the decoy's beaks and nibbled at their wooden bellies. We could only imagine what they were thinking about this strange island. Puffins had returned!

The unbanded puffin was a mystery. Was it a bird from Machias Seal Island or Matinicus Rock? Or perhaps even one of our few fledglings that disappeared on Egg Rock without being banded? How and where did they pair up? They were spotted repeatedly over the next couple of weeks by fishing boats and to the delirious cheering and applause of Hog Island campers on field trips that circled Egg Rock.

To our knowledge, no one had ever watched the very beginning of a puffin colony. With luck this "spark" would grow into a thriving community.

Concerned that we had not seen any puffins return during the first four years of the project, I began trying to think like a puffin. I worried that if puffins did return to Egg Rock, they might not come ashore because there were no other puffins on the island. This thought led to creating puffin decoys. Within days of positioning decoys, a puffin landed and took a close look. Photo by Derrick Jackson.

7.

PUFFIN WITH FISH

With the return of the first puffins, I revisited Palmer's *Maine Birds* with fresh eyes. I found accounts that Egg Rock was also once home to a large colony of Common and Arctic Terns. There were a handful that survived the increasing numbers of gulls and nested here as late as 1936 when the

Arctic Terns have the longest migration of any animal, migrating up to 71,000 km (44,000 miles). In Maine they nest with Common Terns. Photo by Derrick Jackson.

Audubon camp opened. There were none left by the 1970s, and they were in decline throughout Maine.

Flocking together, Arctic and Common Terns can chase off gulls and falcons from their nesting colonies. I reasoned that if I could attract these feisty birds, they would help to protect puffins as well as their own families. Photo by Jean Hall.

Terns were not known to have any conflict with puffins, but they were well known to chase off gulls by dive bombing and pecking at them. I reasoned that If we could attract a large number of terns, perhaps they would act as a protective "umbrella" for puffins. If this level of biodiversity worked as I hoped, perhaps this would restore a "balance" that would allow us to one day end the project and let the puffins thrive on their own.

I went back to Donal O'Brien and asked if he would carve us Arctic Tern decoys. He was a busy lawyer, but he made the time to carve me two beautiful tern decoys, one in an incubating posture, the other in an alert pose. Then I started thinking about tern colonies and how noisy they are during the nesting season. Trying to think like a bird led me to also play tern colony courtship sounds. I made a recording of tern calls and played it on a tape player powered by a car battery.

We started the tern decoy and tape effort in April of 1978. Within days, terns started hovering over the loud-speaker, and then 15 landed on the island. I was thrilled beyond words. Some males hovered with fish to offer to potential mates. Some even offered fish to the decoys. Still others tried to copulate (have sex!) with the decoys!

In 1978, I began using tern decoys and Arctic Tern sound recordings with the hope that I could encourage terns to nest again at Egg Rock after an absence of about 40 years. I was amazed when terns began landing with the decoys and some offered food to the decoys. Photo by Stephen Kress.

The terns' arrivals stunned us, given that Arctic Terns can travel 44,000 miles a year in migration from the Northern Hemisphere to the Southern Hemisphere. Somewhere in that 44,000 miles they spared a mile to land on Egg Rock.

Then, in a flash of time, it was mid-July and time to raise another hundred puffin chicks.

Three years after we started attracting terns to Egg Rock, Arctic Terns nested and immediately began chasing gulls away from their chicks. Here, a parent tern provides a meal for a chick. Photo by Kristin Mosher.

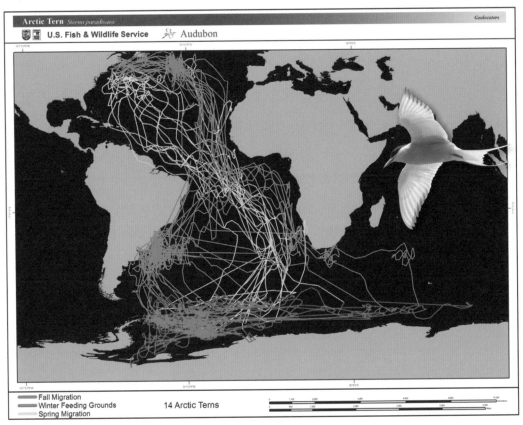

Fall Migration
Winter Feeding Grounds   14 Arctic Terns
Spring Migration

It was well known that Arctic Terns which nest on Maine islands travel to Antarctica for the winter, but until recently, the pathways were unknown. Now, thanks to tiny geolocators attached to Arctic Tern leg bands, Arctic Tern migration routes to Antarctica are better known. This map shows that some of 14 tagged terns from Eastern Egg Rock passed Africa on their way to Antarctica, while others followed a route past South America (green lines). Most winter in the Weddell Sea (red lines) before heading north in spring up the center of the Atlantic Ocean (yellow lines). The map also shows several key migration stop over locations. (indicated by concentrated lines) Map by Maine Coastal Islands National Wildlife Refuge (USFWS). Arctic Tern image by Jean Hall.

In 1979, the famed wildlife documentary Wild Kingdom produced a special about Project Puffin. Richard Podolsky paints a puffin decoy while host, Marlin Perkins observes. Photo by Stephen Kress.

We would put out about a hundred more in 1978, 1979, 1980, and 1981. We were now on an emotional roller coaster.

On the promising side, our efforts were featured on Mutual of Omaha's Wild Kingdom television series.

Returning puffins were also responding to a new gimmick to hold their attention and encourage them to stay longer—a four-sided mirror box. This idea came from my memory of keeping a mirror in the cage of a pet parakeet at my childhood home in Columbus. I hoped the visiting puffins might interact with their reflection in the mirror and stay longer, thus improving the chance that they would meet other feathered puffins.

The mirror was an instant success. We put the mirror near decoys, and when puffins landed among the decoys, they were usually quick to also see the mirror box. They tended to walk around the box, peck at it and often sit down next to it for hours at a time.

To encourage puffins to stay at Egg Rock, I positioned a box with mirrors near the puffin decoys. I hoped that puffins would land near the decoys and then see their reflection in the mirrors. My hunch played out—the puffins were intrigued by their reflections and often sat next to the mirrors for hours where they often met other puffins. Photo by Derrick Jackson.

In 1978, we tallied a record 21 consecutive days of seeing at least one puffin. One day, we finally hit the mark of seeing ten individual puffins in one day. Then 11. By 1979, we were sufficiently encouraged that we were on the road to success that we built a 12-by-12 ft cabin that we called the Egg Rock Hilton. This was the same year that Marlin Perkins, host of Wild Kingdom, produced an hour long special about the Project and wrote in our Egg Rock journal: "The puffin transplant is indeed a wonderful story and evidence has come in to show that it is working . . . Praise the Lord."

The menagerie of life around Egg Rock continued to grow along with puffin numbers. By late August, Diane and Tom saw nine puffins circle the island, as if giving the team a grand send-off for the season. Every part of the seascape was dotted with feathered reminders of southward migration: Common Loons moved south in flocks. Hundreds of Ruddy Turnstones roosted along the shore with a few Red Knots and Sanderlings.

One night the sky was lit up with stars and waves of aurora borealis.

Although we were seeing more puffins, they were not going under the rocks for breeding, and this was a great concern. By 1980, the single-day counts of returning adults hit 23 puffins. In one count, research assistant Diane De-Luca saw at least one banded puffin from each of our 1975, 1976, 1977 and 1978 cohorts.

For the first time, we saw a puffin drop down into the

Egg Rock Hilton. Photo by Pat Wallenbach

crevices under the boulders. We hoped this was the first evidence of scoping out a nest.

By mid July our tern population grew to 150. On one count, we found 170 glorious speckled beige- and olive-colored tern eggs in 72 nests, and chicks were popping up everywhere. Perhaps feeling safe with these numbers of their Arctic cousins, endangered Roseate Terns began showing up.

But there was a bottom line I could not escape. Seven years into the project, we had fledged 630 puffin chicks into the wild. There was still no breeding. Where were those nearly 600 puffins that we raised?

Just as disturbing, we heard that one of our Egg Rock chicks (now five years old,) was breeding on Matinicus Rock, 34 miles away. Did this mean that all our work would only add more birds to an existing colony? I ended 1980 believing we were on the brink of either triumph or becoming a trivial footnote in the annals of fools.

The year 1981 started horribly for environmentalists. New President Reagan appointed a doomsday cabinet who wanted to leave stewardship of the nation's coastlines to top polluting industrial interests. His administration proposed a massive billion-dollar cut to the Department of the Interior, my primary federal partner in Maine seabird conservation.

Because the Atlantic Puffin was not listed as an endangered species, I wondered how much longer I could maintain support for my project. Now, eight years into the project without any evidence of nesting, critics were raising their voice against my project, including Ralph Palmer.

He complained to Roland Clement, Audubon's vice president for science, that puffins would never breed again on Egg Rock. Clement fortunately ignored Palmer, saying it was up to the puffins to decide if they would call Egg Rock home.

The puffins made their decision on July 4, 1981.

On the mainland, Mainers dressed in red, white, and blue lined the streets in town after town for parades of antique cars, marching bands and quirky floats. I might as well have been on a different continent. I was six miles out to sea, hoping for a parade of birds. I was doing a frustrating five-hour stint in a tiny plywood bird blind, sitting on a bucket. I saw no puffins and my loneliness was amplified by a pea soup fog that blocked the sight of land and neighboring islands.

I left the blind at 2 PM to head back to the Egg Rock Hilton and tell research assistant Evie Weinstein it was time for her to take my place. Before I got to the cabin, she exploded out of the fog. She was waving her arms in the contortions of a cartoon traffic cop signaling everyone to proceed simultaneously in all directions. Her whirling limbs prevented her from talking, let

Egg Rock Hilton with Common Tern.
Photo by Bob Butaky.

Eight years into the project, we still had not seen a puffin returning to Egg Rock with fish in its beak. A puffin delivering fish into a rock crevice would be proof that a chick had hatched at Egg Rock. My patience paid off on the 4th of July, 1981 when a puffin suddenly showed up with a beak load of fish, popped into a rock crevice and came up without its catch. Success at last! Puffins were nesting again at Egg Rock after an absence of about a hundred years!
Photo by Derrick Jackson.

alone shouting. What could this be about, on this otherwise grim, almost lifeless day? What could she have seen that launched her into pandemonium?

"Puffin . . . with fish!!!" she finally blurted out.

"Where!?!?!? When!?!?!?" I stammered.

Breathless with excitement, Evie explained that she had been collecting seawater for washing dishes. Like an apparition, a puffin emerged out of the fog and buzzed past her carrying a load of silver fish in its beak.

Evie was so excited, she called the local marine operator, named Marge. Marine radio channels are usually for very basic, dryly delivered navigation information or dire emergencies.

Evie broke protocol and called the operator. Marge asked if it was an emergency. Evie said "No, no, no!" She breathlessly exclaimed with no pause between words, "Puffinwithfishinitsbeak! PuffinbabiesonEasternEggRock! Igottatellsomeonesolcalledyoufirst!'"

Marge responded patiently, "That must have been cool."

We pulled out a spotting scope to scan where Evie had last seen the puffin. But we only saw barren rocks. Several hours passed with no new sightings. Then at 7:40 PM, a puffin sliced out of the fog with its beak packed full of silvery fish. It scrambled over the rocks, then disappeared into a crevice! Fifteen minutes later, it popped up from the crevice, with no fish.

The puffin hopped up onto the rocks and paused near another puffin that appeared to be standing guard. Perhaps it was a mate. The puffin that had come with the fish flew away. Nearly a half-hour later, as dusk darkened the island, the feeding puffin delivered more fish.

This was the day we dreamed of. By the end of 1981, we tallied five breeding pairs of puffins. After a century of absence and eight years that often seemed futile, Evie's three words, "Puffin ... with fish!!!" were the three most important words of my career. For the first time, a seabird was restored to an island where humans had wiped it out.

8.

HERE COMES A BIG ONE!

O ur triumph brought national media attention, including CBS *Sunday Morning*, *National Geographic*, and Public Broadcasting Service's program *Nature*. The narrator for *Nature* was none other than the venerable Roger Tory Peterson, considered the father of modern birdwatching. Decorated by presidents, he is the author of bird guides that are among the most popular in America.

The producers of the show wanted to bring Roger to Eastern Egg Rock because more than fifty years earlier, he had brought Hog Island campers to the island. The theme of the program was to show changes over Peterson's fifty years of birding.

At the time of his visit for the *Nature* documentary, Roger was 81 years old and recovering from surgery. He was a frail version of the birding hero that Irv Kassoy introduced me to when I was a teenager in Columbus, Ohio. While making arrangements to bring him onto Egg Rock, Roger's wife Ginny told me, "Take care of Roger—he is a national treasure."

After they spent several days camping on Eastern Egg Rock, I picked up Roger and the film crew in my 23-foot outboard boat, the Lunda III. We were on our way back to Hog Island where Roger was scheduled to speak to the campers when I suggested that we take a quick visit to Western Egg Rock. My idea was to contrast it with Eastern Egg Rock. While Eastern Egg Rock was alive with a diverse colony of terns and puffins, Western Egg Rock was dominated mostly by gulls—just as Eastern Egg Rock had been before we began Project Puffin.

As we puttered around Western Egg Rock to film it from the water, we noticed waves crashing on the south side of the island, but the seas were relatively calm. Everyone was looking at the island, chatting about birds with their backs to the ocean. I was the first to notice the sea change.

Over my left shoulder a massive wall of green water suddenly blotted the horizon. I shouted, "Here comes a big one!" But it was too late for my warning. In a blurry instant, the crest of a huge rogue wave curled down into our boat. In that moment of capsizing chaos, I thought, "This has never happened before! I've made hundreds of trips down this bay in this boat. How can this be happening now with Roger Tory Peterson on board!" But it was happening. Roger, everyone on board, and all of the equipment were flipped into the frigid water.

Mike Male, the cameraman, went straight to the bottom, weighed down by his lead battery belt. Tangled in cables and still clutching his camera, he probably would not have made it back to the surface without sound recordist, Judy Fieth, quickly diving down to free him of his lead weight. They bobbed to the surface, but they left his $50,000 camera, ruined, on the bottom.

Some of us climbed up on the belly of the capsized boat, but soon we were swept off again into the water. Worried that someone would be trapped under or hit by the tossing boat, we struggled to the shore.

Roger was completely spent. While the rest of us were merely soaked, exhausted, and chilled to the bone, he was bleeding from barnacle scrapes and holding his ribs in pain. Shock from the cold was setting in, and he was shivering. Even with our help, he could barely stagger forward.

We laid Roger down, and Mike huddled next to him to share his body heat. As luck would have it, a camping tent from our wrecked boat floated ashore. We quickly set it up to provide shelter and a windbreak for Roger.

The sun warmed the tent's interior, and we all took turns lying next to our birding hero, talking to him, afraid that if he fell asleep, he might not wake again. His quiet voice was rambling; I feared he was going into shock.

Butterflies were migrating that day. Even in his stupor, Roger noticed the red admirals and monarchs alighting on the tent, backlit by the afternoon sun. While I lay next to him, I heard him ask if these were angels.

Much later, he recounted that he actually thought they were angle wings, a type of beautiful orange butterfly that migrates along the Maine coast. But perhaps he did mean angels, for he went on to tell me that while he was underwater, he thought that he saw Mildred, his first wife. I later learned that his first wife had met a tragic, mysterious end by drowning in this very same Muscongus Bay.

We kept Roger as warm as we could, but the fog was rolling back in and the thought of spending the night on the rock was scary, especially considering Roger's condition. Then we noticed a boat on the horizon. It was the Hardy Boat making its late afternoon puffin cruise from New Harbor to Egg Rock, loaded with observant birders with binoculars. We had built a bonfire on the shore and were hoping that someone would see the smoke and get curious. We were thrilled when we saw the Hardy Boat turn in our direction!

When they realized we were in trouble, they called the Coast Guard to rescue us. A day later, Roger's camera bag

After capsizing at Western Egg Rock, we were thrilled to see the Hardy III coming to our aid, detouring from the evening puffin watching trip to Eastern Egg Rock. When they saw that we were in trouble, they radioed the U.S. Coast Guard which sent a rescue ship. Later, Peterson liked to tell the story of how bird watchers saved his life. Photo by Timothy Healy.

was found floating by a lobster fisherman two miles from Western Egg Rock. His Nikon cameras and a $4,000 telephoto lens were lost or ruined. But the film was in surprisingly good condition in sealed plastic containers. PBS had enough to still do a show.

Peterson spent a few days in the local hospital and then went on to continue inspiring people to care about and save birds. He often told the story about how bird watchers saved his life after a shipwreck on the Maine coast and how the cold-water dunking recharged his love for birds. I was happy that his last visit to Egg Rock did not come at the cost of losing my hero!

Roger Tory Peterson continued to inspire people about birds and conservation for 15 years after his visit to Egg Rock, until his last days at age 96. He helped to share our amazing story and encourage others to see that they too can help birds survive in our human dominated world.

Peterson was not the last to document the seabird comebacks of Project Puffin. Reporters continue to visit Egg Rock to learn about seabirds and what they tell us about their watery world.

From those first five nesting pairs in 1981, the number of puffins at Egg Rock has continued to increase. By 2019, there were 188 pairs nesting at Egg Rock.

Encouraged by the Egg Rock success, I wanted to start a second puffin colony. If I could repeat my success on a separate island, I could make an even stronger case that it was possible to revive lost seabird colonies. Replication is the best way to demonstrate a successful science project.

I chose Seal Island National Wildlife Refuge off of Rockland, Maine (34 miles east of Egg Rock) as my next puffin restoration project because it was once mid-coast Maine's largest puffin colony. Just as on Egg Rock, puffins disappeared here in the mid-1880s from too much hunting for meat and feathers.

With cooperation of David Nettleship and the Canadian Wildlife Service, we transplanted 950 Newfoundland puffin chicks to Seal Island from 1984 to 1989. In most years we moved 200 chicks at a time. Similar to Egg Rock, eight years passed before we saw the first nesting in 1992. Since then the Seal Island puffin colony has grown to about 600 pairs, making it the largest puffin colony in Maine. Today, there are about 1,300 breeding puffin pairs on five Maine islands, including small colonies on Petit Manan Island National Wildlife Refuge and Great Duck Island where puffins started nesting without importing chicks from Canada. Meanwhile, the colony on Machias Seal Island has increased to about 5,000 nesting pairs.

On Matinicus Rock, the island where only a few puffins nested in 1900, the colony has grown to about 500 pairs. Puffins are flourishing here because Project Puffin researchers keep predatory gulls and other predators from taking over the island. This protection has also led to the growth of Maine's largest colony of Razorbills, distant puffin cousins. Common Murres, also puffin relatives, recolonized the island in 2018. In that year, five pairs nested among the puffins, the first to nest on the island since 1883. Like puffins, razorbill and murre ancestors were also hunted for food and

On Matinicus Rock, only about two puffin pairs survived the era of seabird hunting, but those few birds helped to attract other puffins and the colony has continued to thrive with at least 500 pairs nesting here in recent years. The increase is due in part to protection from predators and the addition of some of the Newfoundland puffin chicks that joined this colony. Photo by Stephen Kress.

Murres likely made their decision to nest at Matinicus Rock because of increasing numbers of razorbills and puffins. This gave the murres confidence to pioneer a new colony. Murre decoys and sound recordings also helped build up numbers of murres. Photo by Menno Schaefer via Shutterstock.

feathers. Their return is another example of how people can help to revive lost seabird colonies.

Manx Shearwaters are another seabird success story. These crow-sized cousins of albatross began nesting at Matinicus Rock in 2009. Most Manx Shearwaters nest on the British side of the Atlantic; Matinicus Rock is the only United States outpost for the species. Manx Shearwaters can live up to 50 years and some may fly as many as five million miles in their lifetime. Each year we solve a few more mysteries about these

In 2018, after an absence of about 130 years, at least nine pairs of murres nested, producing at least six chicks at Matinicus Rock. Unlike murres which typically nest on steep cliffs and in much larger numbers, these first colonists chose to nest in rock crevices where they found safety from predatory gulls and ravens. Photo by Frank Mayer.

birds and become all the more amazed by their lives. For example, in 2019 we discovered that Manx Shearwaters nesting at Matinicus Rock fly to the southern tip of South America. Here they find abundant food and avoid Maine's frigid winter months. The following spring they return to their own Matinicus Rock nesting burrows, just as the weather improves.

Manx Shearwaters nest underground at Matinicus Rock, their only known nesting island in the United States. This fuzzy chick is about one month old. When it is ten weeks old, it is old enough to receive a unique leg band from Project Puffin biologists Frank Mayer and Shannon Blake. It will leave without its parents and conduct its first migration, instinctively knowing where to find its winter home. Manx Shearwaters can live 50 or more years, during which time their migrations may cover 8 million km (5 million miles). Photo by Project Puffin staff.

Today, Project Puffin actively manages seabirds on seven Maine islands from southern to mid-coast Maine. In addition to our projects with puffins on Eastern Egg Rock, Seal Island National Wildlife Refuge, and Matinicus Rock, the Project also manages and protects thirty other waterbird species. These include 100% of Maine's endangered Roseate Terns, about half of Maine's endangered Least Terns and most of the state's threatened Arctic Terns and Great Cormorants. Likewise, about 70% of Maine's Common Terns, a species of Special Concern, nest on Project Puffin protected islands.

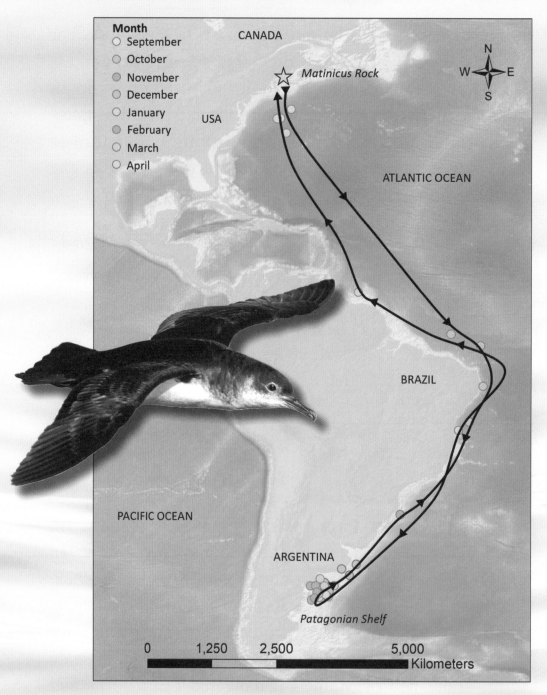

Until recently, it was unknown where Manx Shearwaters spend the winter months. A recent project using geolocators attached to leg bands discovered that the Matinicus Rock Manx Shearwaters travel about 11,250 km (7,000 miles) southward through the Caribbean Sea and then hug the coast of South America until they reach their winter home off of Peninsula Valdes, Argentina. Here they join hundreds of thousands of other Manx shearwaters from eastern Atlantic (European) colonies. This important marine habitat is also home to southern right whales, elephant seals and Magellenic Penguins. Map by Annette Fayet (University of Oxford).

Manx Shearwater by Tony Mills via Shutterstock.

Saving these seabirds is possible because about thirty college-age research assistants (also called seabird stewards and puffineers) live among the seabirds protecting and studying them each summer. Since its beginning, more than 700 early career biologists have taken part in Project Puffin's Maine programs. These include more than 25 young biologists from 15 other countries, many of whom have taken their new knowledge about seabirds back home to help save seabirds.

Each summer more than 10,000 people circle Eastern Egg Rock on tour boats from New Harbor, Boothbay Harbor, and Port Clyde. I often reflect on how the puffin-watching experience has changed. Back in the feather-hunting days, puffin watchers at Egg Rock saw puffins for purely practical purposes of food and feathers.

Today, excited puffin watchers leave the island completely satisfied by taking home photos and memories. Others learn about seabirds and sometimes land on Egg Rock by taking part in the teen birding programs offered by the Hog Island Audubon Camp. A visit to Project Puffin Visitor Center in Rockland is a great way to prepare for these trips. Here, visitors can watch a short video about puffins and meet some of the researchers.

The thrill of visiting Egg Rock is not just about seeing a new species, it is about realizing that something very special happened at this tiny speck of land. It is the first place that people stepped up to influence which seabirds would call an island home. This means we don't have to sit back and witness the loss of more and more species. Some would call this "playing God." I would call it being a responsible steward for life on Earth. Project Puffin demonstrates that people can not only deplete wildlife, but they can also replenish and restore it. The choice is ours. We can make a difference!

Puffins and most seabirds are now protected from hunting in North America, but they face new and even greater threats that require ongoing stewardship. Even on the most remote islands, seabirds feel the influence of people, because everyone and everything is connected by ocean currents and global winds that have no boundaries. Although most people live on land, our influence affects even the most remote places.

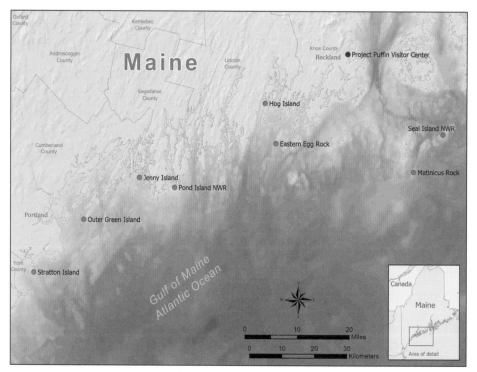

Project Puffin manages seven seasonal field stations on key seabird nesting islands that are home to most of Maine's rare and endangered seabirds. This map also shows the location of the Hog Island Audubon Camp and Project Puffin Visitor Center in Rockland. Map by Bob Houston, U.S. Fish and Wildlife Service.

9.
THE CASE OF THE
MISSING FISH

When Project Puffin began, I tried to catch enough fish to feed the first few puffin chicks, but failed terribly. My lack of fishing success was due partly to my equipment and skill, but I was surprised because the Maine coast was once famous for herring (sardines). Photos of boats loaded with bountiful catches are still widely displayed, though mostly they are black-and-white photos taken long ago. It turns out that those photos of vast herring catches are now only memories—the stuff of museums. Sardine packing plants are closed and herring are comparatively rare.

To feed the puffin chicks, I had to buy small frozen fish such as smelt and silversides from Canada. I couldn't count on catching enough local fish. Happily, puffins are better at catching fish than I am—but in some years they too are now having trouble.

Dark Harbor Fishermen. Painting by N. C. Wyeth, 1943. Atlantic Herring were once abundant along the Maine coast. From about 1870 to 1950, thousands of workers packed sardines (small herring) in 50 canneries. The last cannery closed in 2010 as herring stocks declined. Photo by Daderot (Public domain.)

Puffin fishing success is related to local ocean climate, and this is rapidly changing. Climate change was never mentioned in the early 1970s when I started to think about bringing puffins back to Egg Rock. But understanding climate change now helps me see why puffins sometimes struggle to find enough fish for their chicks.

Today we know that climate change is affecting plants and animals in ways that aren't immediately obvious. Climate describes conditions in an entire region over a time span of thirty years or more. Some people confuse climate with weather. I find it helpful to think of weather as outdoor conditions on one day at one place. Weather forecasts can tell you what clothing to wear for a day, but weather reports tell us little about climate. Understanding climate means looking at temperature and weather records over a long period and in a large area.

Climate scientists are helping seabird biologists understand why fish are missing. One of the surprising discoveries is that water temperature in the Gulf of Maine is warming faster than 99 percent of the world's oceans, a pattern that has continued over many decades. This change is not so obvious if one just puts a hand into the coastal water. It still feels frigid to the touch and too cold for swimming on most days. But little fish respond to the difference. This is important because a warming ocean can affect the distribution, abundance and behavior of the fish that are key foods for seabirds and other ocean predators.

I used to think that because Egg Rock was an island, I didn't have to consider how changes elsewhere might affect the outcome of Project Puffin. Now I realize that Egg Rock is connected to everything, and that climate change affects this little island in very big ways.

Climate change is caused by the increasing amounts of "greenhouse gases" (especially carbon dioxide) building up in Earth's atmosphere, the layer of air that surrounds Earth. Worldwide, the amount of carbon dioxide in the atmosphere has increased to just over 400 parts per million (ppm), the highest concentration in at least 800,000 years.

Most climate warming gases come from burning fossil fuels such as gasoline, coal, and heating oil in cars, trucks, homes and factories. These gases trap heat from the sun near

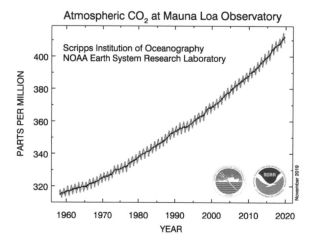

Proof of the growing amount of CO_2 in Earth's atmosphere comes from the top of Mauna Kea, home of the Mauna Loa Observatory sponsored by NOAA and Scripps Institute of Oceanography. Since 1960, the proportion of CO_2 in the atmosphere has continued to increase, reaching more than 400 parts per million in 2020.

Earth's surface. While a certain level of greenhouse gases is necessary to insulate our earth from the cold of space, the high concentrations today trap too much energy from sunlight. As a result, the average temperature on earth is rising. The effect is similar to how heat from sunlight builds up inside of a car on a hot summer day.

This global warming has already raised Earth's average air temperature by 1.1°C (2.0°F) since 1880. Climate scientists predict that if Earth warms more than 1.5°C (2.7°F), it will be a point of no return for many of Earth's plants and animals, especially those with already small ranges in polar regions and mountaintops. Animals like polar bears and Snowy Owls have nowhere to go. Puffins are also at risk, and they are already declining throughout much of their range because of climate change.

There may already be irreversible damage to some fragile and rare plants and animals, but the effect will be much worse if Earth's average temperature rises by 2°C (3.6°F) or more. For example, almost all coastal corals will be lost if the average air temperature increases by 2°C. This would be an enormous loss to Earth's living treasures. Even though corals cover only 0.1% of the ocean floor, they host more than one quarter of all marine fish species.

Average temperature increases of 1°C may seem very small, considering that air temperature in some places can easily swing by 20°C (36°F) in a day. Yet a 1°C increase is a global average which means many areas are warming far more than 1°C. The global ocean has absorbed 90% of the excess heat trapped by greenhouse gases since 1970.

It is more than chance that nine out of ten of the hottest years on record have occurred since 2005. Temperature change alone is not the only effect of climate change. Warmer temperatures bring increases in rain, droughts, supersize hurricanes, and floods—all linked to changes in how moisture moves through the atmosphere.

Until recently, I had not noticed changes at Egg Rock, but now I see worrisome signs that Maine puffins are at risk of becoming a climate casualty. Usually climate effects in the ocean are out of sight and out of mind to most people, but not to puffins. They can tell us about what is happening to their ocean home by observing the kinds of food that they bring home to their chicks and their success fledging young.

Warming is also causing sea level to rise as warmer water expands and melts ice at both poles. Already, the global average sea level has risen about eight to nine inches since

1880. At this rate, by 2100, the global average increase will be more than two feet. Combined with larger storms, sea level rise will be a big problem, especially for seabirds that nest on low elevation islands such as Eastern Egg Rock where the highest ground is just 17 feet above the high tide. World-wide, flooding of coastal cities and entire islands where people live should be a great concern, though many still prefer to think climate change is not real or won't affect them.

Ocean acidity has increased by 30% since 1880 when people began burning increased amounts of oil and gas as well as coal. This is because as the amount of carbon dioxide in the atmosphere rises, the oceans absorb much of it. When carbon dioxide mixes with seawater, it forms carbonic acid, just like soda water. This weak acid can make it difficult for many kinds of plankton to thrive.

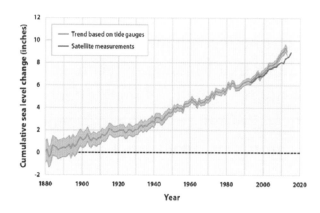

Cumulative changes in sea level for the world's oceans since 1880, based on a combination of long-term tide gauge measurements and recent satellite measurements. The shaded band shows the likely range of values, based on the precision of methods used. Data sources: CSIRO, 2016;3 NOAA, 20164

Abundant, healthy plankton are the main food for small fish that feed seabirds and other ocean predators like big fish, whales, seals and sea turtles. The kind of plankton is also important, as some plankton are much more nutritious than others. Little fish can follow patches of plankton, but this often takes them far from nesting islands or into deeper waters. Understanding how plankton populations are changing species, abundance, timing, and distribution begins to explain about the missing fish.

As ocean warming melts ice at both the Arctic and Antarctic at increasing rates, cold, fresh meltwater affects the ocean currents that warm and cool the planet. We are seeing some of these effects now at Egg Rock. Melting is especially rapid in the Arctic, which may be completely ice-free by the year 2035. The melting water is messing with the ocean currents that make the Gulf of Maine so

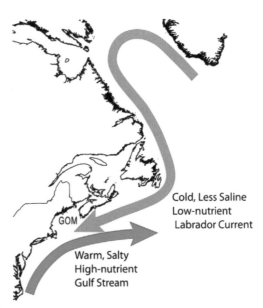

The Gulf of Maine (GOM) sits at a crossroads of influence from major current systems from the north (the Labrador Current) and south (the Gulf Stream). These current systems affect water conditions along the edge of the continent, and thus waters that enter into the Gulf of Maine. How the two systems interact and vary over time is a topic of much study. Map credit: David Townsend.

special. Melting ice from the Arctic Ocean and Greenland is diluting the typically salty water and weakening the southward-flowing Labrador Current.

Previously, the powerful southward-flowing Labrador Current was the dominant water source influencing the Gulf of Maine, but the current has weakened in recent years. Now, warm water "eddies" from the south, sometimes enter the Gulf of Maine. These slugs of warm water are called "ocean heat waves" and they may last for five or more days. They are bad news for cold water plankton, fish and seabirds, including puffins. Worldwide, marine heatwaves have doubled in frequency since 1982 and are increasing in intensity and frequency.

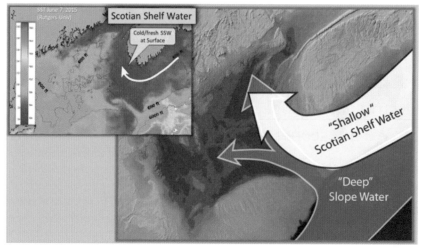

Cold water from the north enters the Gulf of Maine as surface water. At greater depths, water enters from the continental slope, and consists of varying proportions of northern (colder) and southern (warmer) water. Annual variation in these currents greatly influences puffins and other fish-eating wildlife. Puffin colonies occur in the coldest water region of the Gulf of Maine, indicated upper left by the dark blue. Map credit: David Townsend.

These changes are upsetting the unique swirl of cold water that supports northern birds such as puffins and Arctic Terns at the southernmost end of their North American breeding limits.

The summers of 2012 and 2013 may offer a view into the future about how these changes will play out for puffins. In those years, a strong ocean heat wave swept into the Gulf of Maine. Water temperatures near Maine puffin nesting islands usually hover between highs of 13 to 18°C (50s to mid-60s°F). In 2012, summer sea surface temperatures set an all-time record by approaching 21°C (70°F), nearly 4 degrees higher than normal.

Humans can barely perceive a four-degree difference in air temperature, but four degrees is a huge shift for the cold-water fish that puffins eat. Faced with such temperatures, cold water fish like Atlantic herring and white hake move to deeper water and farther from the nesting islands. There, in deeper water, they find comfortable temperatures and the kinds of plankton they need for food.

Puffins, however, usually find most of their food in the upper 15 meters (50 feet) of water. They can't efficiently gather enough food in deeper water or fly more than about 40 kilometers (25 miles) to find a meal for their chick. Deeper dives and longer flights just require too much energy. Unlike fish, puffins are locked to land because they need to lay an egg in a dry island habitat. Finding such places near abundant fish can be challenging. When there are not enough fish near a nesting island, parent puffins may take a summer off from egg-laying to look after themselves.

The heat wave effects were very dramatic in 2012 and extended through the summer of 2013. In the 15 prior years, from 1997 to 2011, the number of breeding puffins on Egg Rock grew steadily upward from twenty pairs to a then-record 123 pairs. The heatwave of 2012-2013 not only chased away the puffins' pre-ferred fish, it attracted butterfish and moonfish northward from the mid-Atlantic coast. These round-bodied fish are usually too large for puffin chicks to swallow. Sadly, many pufflings starved.

Butterfish tend to show up more in puffin diet during warm water summers. They increase in numbers when warm water enters the Gulf of Maine. Butterfish are a problem for young puffins because their round shape makes them difficult for the chicks to swallow.
Photo by Derrick Jackson.

For the first time in a quarter century, the number of breeding pairs on Egg Rock dropped, from 123 to 104 pairs. Other puffin islands suffered even more. The number of breeding pairs dropped by more than half on Petit Manan Island, from 104 in 2009 to 47 pairs in 2013. At Seal Island and Matinicus Rock, puffin parents in 2013 fledged only one of every ten chicks, compared to eight out of ten chicks in good years. We worried that this might become the new normal.

We were relieved to see that puffin numbers rebounded with cooler waters in 2014, 2015 and 2017. Then, in 2018, we had the strangest year in the history of the project.

The summer began with great promise with cool water and record numbers of nesting puffins. Then in mid-July, temperatures soared very close to the 2012 record as a big heat wave gripped the Gulf of Maine. With the increase in ocean temperature, puffin parents suddenly could not find food for their chicks. Starvation set in and researchers found many dead puffin chicks.

Given what happened in 2012, we readied ourselves for a grim end to the summer. But in mid-August, a time that most puffins typically migrate to their winter homes, the surface waters cooled as dramatically as they had risen back in July. With the passing of the ocean heat wave and a return to cooler water, forage fish reappeared as suddenly as they had disappeared when the water warmed.

Those puffin parents that were still trying to feed chicks suddenly found plenty of food within reach and started making up for lost time. Some puffin parents stayed a full three weeks longer than usual and fed their chicks up to 10 times in a day in contrast to just 1-3 feedings a day in the warm water starvation period. Instead of migrating, some kept feeding their chicks into September.

Puffins continue to amaze me by their adaptability. I once thought they were specialists, feeding on only a few kinds of fish, but now I see that they are able to quickly adapt to whatever small fish (squid, shrimp or even octopus) they can find in the right size range. This adaptability gives me hope that if we can limit the amount of carbon dioxide in the air and leave enough small fish in the water, puffins may be able to adapt to the changes.

Enlightened fishing policies that leave more fish in the sea will help puffins and other marine animals adapt to climate change. When puffins first started nesting on Egg Rock and Seal Island, they fed their chicks mostly white hake and Atlantic herring, both cold-water fish. But about 70 percent of herring along the Maine coast are taken for lobster bait, and both herring and white hake are vulnerable to warming waters. Yet that has not stopped the puffin's comeback. Happily, they are finding new kinds of fish to make up the difference. There is also still time to change fishery regulations to recognize that fish need protection too and that people can drive their numbers to dangerously low populations.

Haddock is one of the best examples of how this can work. This popular fish, a favorite for "fish and chips," was once overfished in the Gulf of Maine. Now haddock is carefully managed and serves as a heartening comeback story. Local fishers and puffins are both benefitting. Little haddock (less than one year old) now make up more than half of the food fed to puffin chicks in some years. Ten years ago, haddock was unknown in the diet of Maine puffins. This is the kind of adaptability that will determine which animals will remain in a warming climate. It also points to the importance of maintaining a diverse ecosystem with many species that can adapt to climate change.

Saving the haddock gives me hope that we can make changes now that can help puffins adapt to climate change and that taking care of the small fish is just as important as taking care of the puffins. There is still time to act, but we must all do our part and encourage parents and friends to do their part as well by eating sustainably harvested fish.

It was easy to see how birds died at the hands of the feather hunters. The new threat from climate change is even greater because it affects all life on Earth, including people. It comes down to the reality that we are killing our only home by warming our atmosphere and oceans. Climate change is not a gamble on science predictions, it is a certain path to a more depleted planet, where it will be more difficult for people and wildlife to thrive.

Puffins are safe from hunting in most places, yet they are still at risk throughout most of the world. They are at risk in Europe from the multiple effects of climate change, overfishing, pollution and predators such as rats, mink and cats. As recently as 2012, the Atlantic puffin was so abundant, the International Union for the Conservation of Nature considered it a "Species of Least Concern" on its Red List. Today, it is listed as "Vulnerable" worldwide and "Endangered" in Europe. This is because Europe has more than 90 percent of the world's estimated 12-14 million Atlantic Puffins, but its population is on track to decline by up to 79 percent by 2065.

In the Pacific, the Tufted Puffin is undergoing a similar struggle. Its global population is estimated at 3.5 million birds. But its numbers off the coasts of Washington, Oregon and California have crashed from 30,000 to 4,000 over the last thirty years. Even in wild Alaska, several Tufted Puffin starvation and die-off events since 2014 have resulted in the deaths of thousands of birds in the remote Bering Sea. Federal scientists believe the die-offs were triggered by the "broad-scale ecosystem change" of warming waters forcing fish out of range of nesting colonies. No place is safe from the climate crisis.

These broad-scale threats are hitting puffins just as we are broadening our understanding of their whereabouts in the eight months when they are not breeding. The winter home of Maine puffins was a mystery until 2015 when we attached tiny devices called "geolocators" to puffin leg bands. These tiny tags revealed that most puffins have a two-part migration. In mid-August some leave Maine and head north to the Gulf of St. Lawrence and coast of Labrador. Then in mid-winter they head south to the outer Gulf of Maine and the edge of the continental shelf about 130 miles southeast of Cape Cod.

(Left) Geolocators are tiny tracking devices that determine location by comparing length of day with time of year. Photo by Scott Hall.
(Right) Puffins wear the tiny tags attached to leg bands. Photo by Nathan Banfield.

Those waters include canyons larger than the Grand Canyon and the largest mountains in Eastern United States. This region of deep canyons and underwater mountains (called seamounts) is an important home for whales, turtles, deep sea corals and other seabirds. It is such an important environment that President Barack Obama designated the area the Northeast Canyons and Seamounts National Monument in 2016.

Puffin researcher Caroline Poli managed to capture a tagged puffin. Data from the geolocater showed where the puffin had traveled during the previous year. Photo by Nathan Banfield.

The wonders of the Monument remain largely unexplored. Scientists continue to find additional species previously unknown for this new protected area. This is an example of how protecting ocean habitat is just as important as protecting nesting islands because everything is connected. What people do in one place always effects life elsewhere.

Some conservationists suggest that to truly protect sea life, thirty percent of the world's oceans should receive protection. This should include known areas where seabirds, marine animals and invertebrates such as corals thrive. Such areas can also serve as sanctuaries not only for seabirds and marine animals, but for ocean fish that otherwise are pursued without safe places to reproduce. Fish are wildlife too, and they need more friends.

The discovery of the puffin's winter home is just one example of the new things learned from our long term study of puffins and other seabirds. These discoveries demonstrate that when it comes to saving seabirds, what happens away from nesting islands is just as important as what happens at the nesting place. It is straightforward to protect puffin breeding habitat, but we are just now learning where seabirds spend their non-nesting months. With the advent of increasingly tiny tracking devices, it is a very exciting time to be a seabird biologist!

Just as brave people decided to fight off the feather hunters, it is now time to pass responsible laws and make the right personal decisions to fight climate change. We can all turn off lights that are not in use, eat locally grown foods, eat sustainably harvested fish, and reduce one-time use plastics. Small actions can add up to slow the release of greenhouses gases, protect fish and keep oceans clean. Every action is an opportunity to explain to someone else why we need to act now. But of course, individual actions can only take us so far. We need policies to change, not only locally but also nationally and worldwide.

Even though 95% of scientists are convinced that Earth's climate crisis is caused by humans, many people still refuse to consider this a serious problem or one caused by humans. Too often, climate deniers reject the call for urgent action.

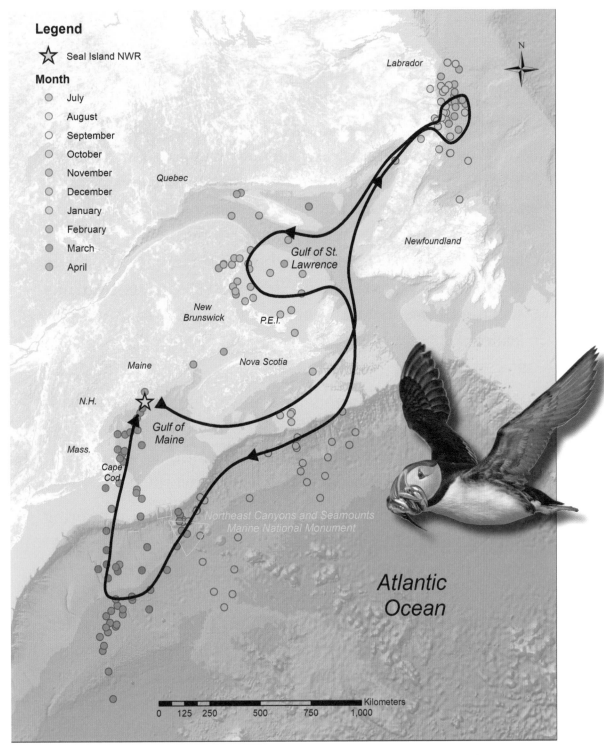

Legend

⭐ Seal Island NWR

Month

○ July
○ August
○ September
○ October
○ November
○ December
○ January
○ February
○ March
○ April

Labrador

Quebec

Newfoundland

Gulf of St. Lawrence

New Brunswick

P.E.I.

Maine

Nova Scotia

N.H.

Gulf of Maine

Mass.

Cape Cod.

Northeast Canyons and Seamounts Marine National Monument

Atlantic Ocean

Kilometers
0   125   250   500   750   1,000

Because puffins are rarely seen from land in winter, their winter home was unknown. Now, tiny geolocators attached to leg bands are revealing the mysteries of this migration. Usually, puffins leave their nesting colonies in late July or by mid-August. About 5% of the birds travel north, making it all the way to Labrador, before returning south to the Gulf of St. Lawrence. On the final leg of their winter travels, they usually return to the edge of the continental shelf where they spend time in the Northeast Canyons and Seamounts Marine National Monument and Gulf of Maine before heading back to Maine nesting islands like Seal Island NWR. Most Maine puffins have shorter winter migrations, staying in the Gulf of Maine and the Marine Monument. Map by Mark Baran.

Yet I find new hope about our chances of holding the line against climate change.

Young people are making their voices heard — and heard loudly—through social media and public protests. These actions are catching the attention of policy makers, and some are coming up with creative plans. Bottom-up movements by enough people can tip enlightened leaders to take action at all levels of government. The greatest and most lasting social movements start from the street, not from political leaders.

There are many examples such as civil rights, women's rights, and LGBTQ rights that prove change is possible if enough people care and make their cares known. Now is the time to preserve our climate and our world as we know it. Everyone has a right to a living, healthy world.

It would be a tragedy to have worked so hard to bring puffins back to Maine just to let them be a casualty of reckless climate change policies and overfishing. The little fish that puffins need to survive are missing because people took too many and polluted the commons of our air and water. The fish that remain are moving deeper and farther from the coast, but they will come back if we do the right things. Puffins are telling us there is a better way. There is still time to listen and take action. Nature is resilient if we do our part.

10.

SEABIRD SUPER HEROES

A casual visit to a coastal beach can give one the impression that there are plenty of seabirds—but the gulls and others that flock at beaches are just a few of the 359 seabird species. Most seabirds live far from beaches and human communities. Yet these far-off seabirds are the ones most feeling the pain of our impact on the natural world.

About half of all seabird species are declining. Globally, one third are threatened with extinction. Invasive predators such as cats and rats, entanglement in fishing nets, and climate change that reduces the fertility of the oceans are the main reasons for these declines. Overfishing, excessive hunting, and pollution are also huge threats. Most species face multiple threats. Against this dangerous, daunting backdrop, how can Project Puffin help?

I remember the stinging words of my critics when I first suggested bringing puffins back to Egg Rock. They said "Why worry about puffins? There are millions in Iceland— it's more important to save the endangered species." Of course, it is important to save endangered species because extinction is tragically final. Yet by saving puffins, we have developed tools that can help save endangered seabirds and reduce risks to many other species.

Too often, human activities result in the loss of nesting colonies and shrinking nesting ranges. This leads to very small remaining populations that are vulnerable to extinction. About 20% of all seabird species have only 5,000 or fewer nesting pairs. The chances of survival are further reduced if a species is restricted to just one nesting island. Then the old saying "all of the eggs are in one basket" becomes tragically true. Worldwide, nineteen of the world's most threatened seabirds nest on just one island.

Fostering more seabird nesting colonies within historic ranges is one of the best ways to guard against disasters such as oil spills, predator invasions and effects of climate change from rising waters and dwindling food supplies. More colonies spread risk, giving the species resilience to rebound from disasters. The idea of helping seabirds make smart decisions on where to nest has much broader application than I first thought.

Originally, I thought only about bringing puffins back to an island where people had hunted too many for food and feathers. But now I realize that the methods we invented to bring back the puffins can help seabirds worldwide by spreading risk to multiple nesting colonies. Every year I hear about new projects using decoys or translocating seabird chicks. I've kept a list and know of at least 64 seabird species in 16 countries where people are using Project Puffin methods to help create new colonies.

The first use of social attraction on the Pacific coast was at a scary location just south of San Francisco called Devil's Slide Rock. It's scary because of its steep, slippery walls that serve as a barrier to any animal that might climb it. That is probably why it became such an important nesting island for Common Murres. Murres nested atop the 900-foot tall rock by the thousands until 1986. That year, the Apex Houston barge broke up along the coast, spilling crude oil near Devil's Slide Rock. About 9,000 seabirds were killed, including 6,000 Common Murres.

Common Murres.
Photo by Jane Hall.

After the spill, no murres returned for a decade. Then Harry Carter, a California seabird biologist who had heard about Project Puffin, called me to ask if I thought decoys and sound recordings could help. He offered me a trip to see the location, which I happily accepted.

Soon I was standing on a cliff looking down at Devil's Slide Rock. It was a foggy day, but I still remember the green mountains of water that were rolling against the base of the Rock, throwing foaming spray halfway up the steep cliffs. Against the roar of waves, I asked Harry if this was a typical day. He looked me in the eye and said: "I've seen worse." These waves

About 6,000 Common Murres died in the tragic oil spill from the Apex Houston barge in 1986. In that year, Common Murres stopped nesting at Devil's Slide Rock, a 900' tall sea stack in central California. Biologists launched a valiant restoration project using decoys and audio recordings in 1996 to encourage murres to recolonize the rock. Several pairs responded immediately by nesting among the decoys and now the colony has grown to about 3,000 nesting murres. Photo by Michael Parker.

were huge to me, and it was hard to imagine landing people on the island. I didn't know that Harry was a master rubber boat driver. His skill turned out to make all the difference.

Harry knew just how to ride the rollers in his Zodiac boat and when to dash in, between the waves, to land biologists. He also knew biologists like Mike Parker who were expert mountain climbers. These were all new skills to this East Coaster who was more familiar with rowing boats and landing on less frightening islands. With Harry's confidence that landing was possible and that climbers could scale up the slippery cliffs, I began thinking about what it would take to entice murres back to Devil's Slide Rock. The only

Mike Parker, first director of the Devil's Slide Rock Murre Restoration Project sets out some of the 400 decoys that he and his team secured onto the top of Devil's Slide Rock in 1992. Photo by Stephen Kress.

missing part was funding, but that is where environmental lawyers signed on to the cause. They successfully argued that the birds were legally protected and the barge owners were responsible for restoring them.

The resulting settlement provided 5.4 million dollars for murre restoration. No one had previously attempted to use decoys and audio recordings of murre calls to help start a murre colony, but the concept was solid based on our work with puffins. After all, murres are highly colonial members of the puffin family. Like puffins, they nest in colonies for safety from predators. Because murres are highly vocal at the colonies, we decided to also provide colony sounds as we had done with terns, another vocal seabird. The concept was promising, but I assumed it would take years to succeed. As usual, there were many who thought it would never work.

Common Murres with chick. Photo by Jordi Jornet via Shutterstock.

Finally, in 1996, a team that included project leader Mike Parker, Harry Carter, myself and longtime Project Puffin colleague "Seabird" Sue Schubel scaled the rock to install decoys, mirrors, and solar-powered audio soundtracks. Climbing the rock was just as scary as I expected. On my first climbing trip, we found higher waves than expected, so we waited for an occasional calm spell. Then Harry would dash in to the landing rock, scream "Jump!" and then back away quickly. One at a time we hopped out and then climbed the ropes to the top.

We were shocked when Sue reported that a murre landed with the decoys the day after they were installed. Breeding occurred later that first year, and the colony today has grown to 3,000 murres. The quick response was likely because there were still some living murres from

Devil's Slide Rock 2012 (after restoration)

the original colony that had a memory of the place and only needed the encouragement of decoys, mirrors and sound to nest there again.

This project is especially rewarding because ongoing active management is no longer necessary. I was happy to see the active part end because, even with Harry's capable help, it was very dangerous.

Decoys and audio recordings have also helped Japanese conservationists start new colonies of endangered Short-tailed Albatross. By far the largest colony of Short-tailed Albatross was on Torishima, an active volcanic island in the Izu Island group. Millions of these huge, beautiful birds once nested on Torishima Island and several other Japanese islands. Tragically, by 1900, almost all of the birds had been killed by feather hunters who used their soft down feathers to stuff pillows and mattresses. It took about 100 albatross to stuff one mattress!

Short-tailed Albatross pair.
Photo by Hiroshi Hasegawa.

By 1900 about 5 million Short-tailed Albatross had been slaughtered, nearly driving this great bird to extinction.

Only a few albatross that nested on the steepest slopes of Torishima Island survived the feather hunting massacre. While the birds were saved from the hunters, this habitat is a risky place to incubate an egg, as winds often bury the eggs

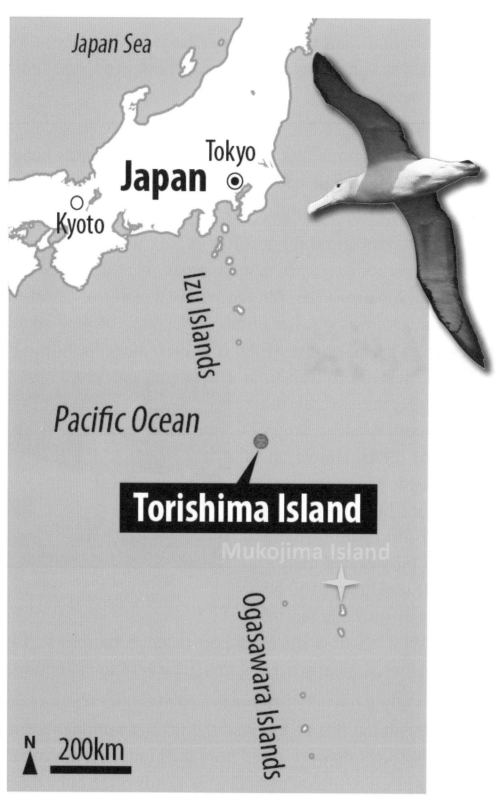

Japan Sea

Tokyo

Japan

Kyoto

Izu Islands

Pacific Ocean

Torishima Island

Mukojima Island

Ogasawara Islands

N
200km

©2018 The Sankei Shimbun / JAPAN Forward

Hunting of Short-tailed Albatross from Ogasawara Island, about 1905.

and chicks with ash, and it is only a matter of time until the volcano erupts again. Risk of the next eruption is so great that the island has remained abandoned since 1902, when an eruption killed 125 albatross hunters.

Short-tailed Albatross are now protected from hunting. In 1962, Japan gave the bird the title of "Special Natural Monument." One of the bird's greatest friends is a soft-spoken biology professor from Toho University named Dr. Hiroshi Hasegawa. After stepping foot on the island for the first time in 1977, he dedicated his life to the study and conservation of Short-tailed Albatross. When he discovered

that the birds were having very low nesting success in the steep, ashy habitat at the top of the volcano, he organized a habitat improvement project, planting grasses to give the birds protection.

Installing decoys at Torishima Island, Japan. Photo by Horoshi Hasegawa.

He also used social attraction to encourage some of the birds to nest on flat habitat lower on the island, where they would have a greater chance of fledging their chicks. He set out fifty life-like decoys with recordings of albatross calls in 1992 and added another 45 decoys in 1993. His great patience was rewarded by one pair nesting among the decoys in 1995. This loyal pair returned every year and produced a chick. But no other albatross joined the decoy colony.

It took ten years before a second pair nested with the decoys, a reminder of how important patience is when hoping to start a seabird colony. This is especially true for albatross, as they can live for seventy or more years, and are usually eight or nine years old when they nest for the first time.

About five million Short-tailed Albatross were killed in Japan in the 1800s for feathers to stuff mattresses and pillows. This excessive hunting nearly drove the birds to extinction. Decoys and audio recordings have helped to start new colonies and rebuild the population. Now about 1,000 pairs nest at Torishima Island, but it is an active volcano. Albatross decoys and a sound system helped to encourage Short-tailed Albatross to pioneer a new colony at Torishima Island on flat, stable habitat where they were safer from being buried in ash. Photo by Hiroshi Hasegawa.

The decoy colony continues to gain popularity. Young produced on the volcanic slopes are moving down to the decoy colony to nest, enticed by the decoys and increasing numbers of real birds. By 2017, at least 274 pairs were nesting where Dr. Hasegawa set up decoys. Here they are enjoying greater nesting success than those that continue to nest on the windy volcano summit. On Dr. Hasegawa's 123rd visit to the island in 2017, he found 921 nesting pairs. If the volcano erupts, however, much of this progress will be lost. This is an extreme case of too many eggs in one very dangerous basket.

To spread some of the risk to a non-volcanic island, Dr. Tomohiro Deguchi, then of the Yamashina Institute for Ornithology, began a translocation project in 2008. This was similar to the way I moved puffin chicks from Newfoundland to Maine. Mukojima Island is an historic nesting site where, like Torishima Island, feather hunters killed the last albatross in the late 1880s. Dr. Deguchi arranged for a helicopter to move chicks from the rim of the volcano on Torishima Island and flew them to Mukojima Island in the Ogasawara Islands, 350 km (220 miles) to the southeast. At Mukojima, decoys and sound recordings helped to give chicks the

Albatross were brought by helicopter from Torishima Island to Mukojima Island Here, they are looking at their new home from artificial nests in carrying cases. Photo by Tomohiro Deguchi.

look and sound of an active colony while caregivers fed the chicks. In the years following the translocations, researchers resighted 37 of the 69 juvenile albatross. Twenty-four visited both the release site (Mukojima) and 32 visited their homeland on Torishima.

Nine pairs returned to Torishima where they hatched, and much to everyone's excitement two pairs have nested at Mukojima, founding a new colony! The first of these pairs includes a transplanted chick from Torishima and an unbanded mate. This pair received congratulations from around the world when they hatched an egg in 2016. They enjoyed similar success in each of the next three years. Now a second pair is also nesting. This project proves that it is possible to restore historic albatross colonies at new islands—an important first because many albatross are in need of more colonies. Now the method is also helping start

Unlike puffin chicks that would pick up whole fish from the ground, young albatross needed hand-feeding for several months from a young age until they were ready to fledge. (close-up view on the right) Photos by Tomohiro Deguchi.

new colonies of Chatham Island Albatross in New Zealand and Laysan and Black-footed Albatrosses in Hawaii.

The social attraction method of using decoys and audio recordings was also used in the Columbia River estuary in the Pacific Northwest to lure Caspian Terns away from endangered salmon. The birds had learned that hatchery-raised salmon were easy to catch on their migration down river to the ocean. Somehow, news about this great abundance of food spread rapidly among west coast Caspian Terns. In a few years, most of the Caspian Terns in Western U.S. came together to form the world's largest nesting colony on Rice Island.

Caspian Terns are very capable fish-eating birds. Young salmons made up most of the diet of Caspian Tern chicks in the late 1990s when a large colony on Rice Island in the Columbia River ate millions of young salmon on their way to the Pacific Ocean.
Photo by Tracey Heimberger via Shutterstock.

By the late 1990s, the Rice Island Caspian Terns were eating about 12 million young salmon each year. This outraged people who were trying to rebuild salmon populations and save endangered salmon species. With the discovery of how many fish were being eaten, there were soon proposals to kill the terns. Yet the main reasons for declining salmon were overlooked. It was easier to blame the terns than the dams that block the migration of the fish and clear-cutting forests that result in soil erosion, covering salmon eggs with silt.

Hearing about the threats to the terns, two enterprising biologists stepped up with a creative solution. Dr. Dan Roby and Dr. Don Lyons heard about the successful attraction of Common Terns to Egg Rock and wondered if the use of decoys and sound recordings might also help Caspian Terns in the Columbia River. Their team hatched a plan to clear the shrubs and grasses off of part of East Sand Island, a former Caspian Tern nesting site located about 15 miles downstream from Rice Island in the mouth of the river. They hoped that if the terns moved from Rice Island to East Sand Island, they would find other kinds of fish to eat and they would eat fewer salmon.

They also knew that the terns were too crowded on Rice Island for their own good. The colony had grown to nine thousand pairs by 1998, which was about two-thirds of all Caspian Terns in western North America. Again, too many eggs in one basket! But how could they

Caspian Tern decoys with decoy eggs.
Photo by Daniel Roby.

remove the shrubs and grasses? Dan had an idea—call in the Marines. Luckily, it turned out that the Marines were

Caspian Terns with decoys and sound speakers at East Sand Island.
Photo by Daniel Roby.

looking for just such a place to train with their bulldozers. In just a few days, trainees cleared the shrubs and grasses that had taken fifteen years to grow up since the Caspian Terns last nested at East Sand Island.

Meanwhile, Dan and Don were busy at Rice Island working to make the habitat less appealing. They planted fast growing winter wheat and put up temporary fences to break up the bare sand. Then they placed about 400 Caspian Tern decoys and broadcast audio recordings of Caspian Terns in the newly prepared habitat at East Sand Island. The result was spectacular.

Immediately, many of the salmon-eating terns from Rice Island moved to East Sand Island.

There they switched to a diet mainly consisting of herring and anchovies, both abundant near East Sand. This gave the young salmon a chance to migrate down the Columbia

River and out to sea with fewer attacks from terns.

This project demonstrated that social attraction could help to reduce the impact of fish-eating waterbirds on fisheries. Most important, it showed how the method could simultaneously help terns and endangered fish.

The success of that effort led Dan and Don halfway around the world to take part in a project to save one of the world's rarest seabirds, the Chinese Crested Tern. The rediscovery of the bird and the good luck that follows show how chance, innovation and very hard work can help save a species.

Chinese Crested Terns are threatened by egg collectors, egg-eating snakes, rats, habitat loss and typhoons as well as the perils of migrating thousands of miles. For about seventy years it was feared that the Chinese Crested Tern was extinct. Then film maker Liang Chieh made an amazing discovery.

Recognized by their orange bill with a black tip, Chinese Crested Terns were thought to be extinct, but several were found, giving hope that this very rare bird might have a chance of surviving. Diving Chinese Crested Tern photo by Stephen Kress.

In the year 2000, this noted wildlife film maker was filming a documentary about ecotourism in Taiwan. While reviewing film he had taken of a nesting colony of Greater Crested Terns, he discovered that by accident he had filmed three smaller terns with lighter colored backs than the Greater Crested Terns. The smaller birds also had bright orange beaks with black tips. Puzzled by these mystery birds, he searched through his field guides and came to a startling discovery. Could this be the Chinese Crested Tern? The mysterious "Bird of Legend?" When he shared his film, everyone agreed that the three birds were indeed Chinese Crested Terns!

Researcher in cabin remote monitoring decoys and Chinese Crested Terns.
Photo by Stephen Kress.

It is rare to have a second chance when it comes to saving lost birds. What could be done to make sure that these last few birds could thrive and hopefully rebuild the species? Some worried that there were just not enough to create a healthy population. Perhaps there would be genetic problems from inbreeding. Perhaps it was already too late, even though a few birds were still alive. Others recognized that something should be done immediately while there was still a chance to make a difference.

Then an idea came to Dr. Shuihua Chen of Zhejiang Museum of Natural History and Simba Chan of BirdLife International Partnership. They had heard of my research using decoys and sound recordings and wondered if this might work to attract the rare Chinese Crested Terns to a safe nesting island in China. When they contacted me, I suggested that Dan Roby could share how social attraction might help. His experience with Caspian Terns made him a perfect fit for this new project.

The team chose the island of Tiedun Dao in the Zhoushan Archipelago of the coast of Zhejiang Province as the best place to try the experiment. Three hundred tern decoys and two sound systems were installed on the tiny, treeless island in early spring of 2013. Our hope was that we could attract Greater Crested Terns, a larger species with a bright yellow bill, and that they would help to attract the Chinese Crested Terns.

Greater crested and Chinese Crested Terns (with white back and orange beak) sitting near a decoy (right) at Tiedun Dow, China. Photo by Stephen Kress.

The project got off to a slow start when no terns showed up to visit the decoys. It turned out that the sound system was not working. A quick fix and much to everyone's wonder, the sky filled with Greater Crested Terns. They quickly settled down among the decoys. They loved the sound! Among the huge flock were two pairs of Chinese Crested Terns. One of these successfully fledged a beautiful chick. The successful breeding gave encouragement that the rare terns were not showing genetic inbreeding problems.

Since then both the numbers of Chinese Crested Terns and number of tern attracting projects in China have continued to increase. In 2019, about 95 Chinese Crested Terns were observed at four islands from South Korea to China. Together, they produced at least 33 fledgling Chinese Crested Terns.

The African Penguin Relocation Project is one of the most recent projects inspired by Project Puffin. African Penguins numbered 3 to 4 million in the 1800s, but their numbers have declined by 99%. Their downfall began with egg harvesting that took thirteen million eggs from 1900 to 1930. Then guano harvesters mined the soil where the penguins nested, destroying the habitat where they

African Penguins have declined over the last 100 years from several million to only 20,000 pairs mainly because of over fishing of tiny fish and warming waters. Photo by Stephen Kress.

dug underground nesting burrows. Finally, modern threats such as overfishing, warming water from climate change, and oil pollution reduced the species to fewer than 20,000 pairs in South Africa and Namibia. The African penguin is now listed as an endangered species.

African Penguin chick in hand.
Photo by Stephen Kress.

Reduced supplies of sardine and anchovy are the biggest problem, as the fish have shifted to the south and east of most existing colonies. These fish are now farther than the flightless birds can swim for food. As a result, chicks in the western penguin colonies too often die from starvation. Predators such as wild dogs, cats and even leopards attack the survivors, especially when they choose to nest on the mainland rather than on islands.

As part of an effort to hold back extinction, researchers and the South African government are experimenting with fishing bans near penguin habitat.

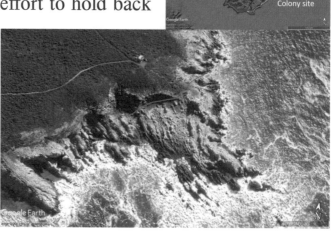

The red lines show the location of the fence to keep predators out of the new attraction location for African Penguins.

African Penguin decoys.
Photo by Christina Hagen.

The latest plan is a chapter from Project Puffin. In 2018, conservationists led by Christina Hagan of Birdlife South Africa installed life-size decoys in a coastal reserve 145 miles east of Cape Town where penguins once nested. Here they have built a fence to keep out predators. They are also playing taped penguin calls, all in hopes of restoring a colony where penguins can find enough fish to feed their young. If these methods are slow to work, the researchers will also move penguin chicks to the new location.

Decoys and audio recordings alone cannot solve the huge threats that penguins and other seabirds face, but they can be part of the solution. Not only can they bring birds closer to food sources, they can also encourage them to nest in places safer from predators. This is the first attempt to use social attraction to help a flightless bird.

The projects described in this chapter demonstrate how methods pioneered in Maine are now helping other seabirds worldwide. I think of this when I remember the critics who told me there was no point in helping puffins because they are still abundant elsewhere. It turns out that helping seabirds start new colonies and thus expand nesting ranges is one of the most useful things that we can do while we also work to hold the line on climate change and protect forage fish.

None of these bold rescue projects would be possible without (human) seabird superheroes. They have several things in common. Seabird heroes thrive on remote islands, have respect but not fear for the sea and are willing to test their creativity and patience to help save seabirds. These are just a few of the inspiring stories about people who really care about animals. If each species of animal on Earth had a hero dedicated to its future, like the heroes described in this chapter, we could do a much better job passing along Earth's wildlife to the next human generation. Will you help?

A four-part restoration plan is taking shape to create a new nesting colony of African Penguins. At a location where small fish are still abundant, researchers will build a fence to keep predators such as leopards out, use decoys and playback calls to attract penguins, translocate chicks, and educate the public about the plight of penguins.
Photo by Stephen Kress.

11.

IS THERE A BALANCE OF NATURE?

As I (Steve) was writing this book with Derrick, his wife, Michelle Holmes, a physician at Harvard University, played devil's advocate. She asked us a simple but piercing question:

"Don't get me wrong. Putting the puffins back is an amazing accomplishment. But if interns have to stay every summer on Eastern Egg Rock, how is it a sustainable project?" Her question gave me pause because it included the word *sustainability*. I have noticed how use of the word is increasing, and yet it lacks a widely accepted meaning.

It usually means "not depleting natural resources to maintain an ecological balance." But that just raises another question. Is there really a *balance of nature*? Is there some plan that keeps one species from gobbling up all of another?

Living on a small seabird island gives one time to think about these things. Especially when it comes to Maine puffins. When we launched our puffin plan in 1973, I hoped to bring back the puffins and eventually take off all signs of people, leaving just the restored puffin colony. I thought I could build the Maine puffin population up to a point where it could survive on its own as it did before European settlement. Now it seems that this is impossible without people protecting puffins during the nesting season. If we stopped the project, gulls and eagles would likely wipe everything out. This reality led me to wondering how puffins once lived on the Maine coast along with their predators in the past. What changed?

Egg Rock looks like a remote, isolated world, but that is an illusion. True, it is separated by miles of salt water from other islands and the mainland. But now I know that there is a complex web of life that connects Egg Rock with other islands, the mainland and all of the living creatures in that web, including people. Now I see that we can't have a sustainable puffin colony without a living and healthy ocean.

People are making huge changes to oceans, but these changes are not so obvious, because oceans seem so vast.

Above: Eastern Egg Rock aerial, 1974. Photo by Stephen Kress. Right: As seen in this 2019 photo, a summer field camp with a cabin and tents for researchers is necessary to protect the Egg Rock puffins. Photo by Richard Podolsky.

After all, together the world's oceans cover 71% of the planet. In many parts of the world, people continue to think of the oceans as an inexhaustible source of water and food and sadly a place to get rid of waste and pollution. At the same time, the number of people who live on the coast has continued to increase, affecting wildlife food, human fisheries, and quality of the water and air.

People cause most environmental problems, but they can also be the source of solutions. It is clear that to help rare and endangered animals thrive, it is not enough to just try to hold the line where we are right now. Some would call active management "playing God." For me, "sustainability" has come to mean taking action on behalf of a planet we have already permanently altered.

On the Maine coast, humans greatly affected seabird populations not only by hunting them but also taking much of their primary food, Atlantic herring. In the same years that feather hunters reduced Maine puffins to just a just a few birds, sardine fishing harvested vast amounts of herring from the coast.

The creation of open landfills, lobstering, and fishing for large bottom fish such as cod and halibut were additional human imposed changes. These activities provided abundant food for gulls, helping them survive throughout the year. This led to vast numbers of gulls that competed for nesting habitat and ate smaller seabirds such as puffins and terns.

Landfills attract gulls throughout the year, but are especially important in the winter when lobster bait and natural foods such as crabs are less available. Terns, puffins and other fish-eating birds cannot feed at landfills and do not benefit from human provided foods, giving the gulls a huge advantage. Photo by Stephen Kress.

Likewise, countless dams on streams and rivers produce electricity, but they also block passage of ocean-going fish into breeding lakes all along coastal Maine. This has greatly reduced the numbers of smelt, alewives, shad and blueback herring that would otherwise be available to feed gulls, eagles, cormorants, salmon, mink, otters and seals. Without the river fish, predators are more likely to turn to seabirds for food.

Even though they sometimes take a puffin or tern, I can see that these predators are just trying to survive and rear their own young. They are very

Herring Gull with Alewife meal.
Photo by Stephen Kress.

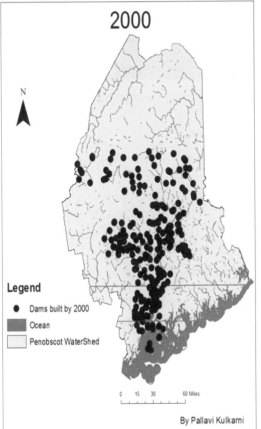

2000

N

Legend

● Dams built by 2000

■ Ocean

□ Penobscot WaterShed

0   15   30   60 Miles

By Pallavi Kulkarni

Dams on the Penobscot River watershed. Before Maine was colonized by Europeans, many kinds of fish migrated up streams to breed in lakes. To create electricity and grain mills for growing human communities, most of Maine's rivers and tributaries were blocked by dams by mid-1800s. By the year 2000, about 190 dams were blocking tributaries of the Penobscot River alone. Similar blockage continues to occur throughout the state. The dams blocked the movement of alewives, shad and blueback herring which are key foods for birds, marine mammals and predatory fish like salmon. Research for map by Pallavi Kulkami.

good at finding the next meal because their lives depend on successful hunting. Without the research assistants living among the seabirds on islands such as Eastern Egg Rock, the gulls would be quick to take up residence again, happy to dine on puffins. Somehow, we need to find ways to shoo away or remove gulls, eagles, herons, owls, mink and otter, while leaving more fish for these fish-eating predators.

This led me to using decoys to attract Arctic Terns back to historic nesting islands. Arctic Terns and their close relatives Common and Roseate Terns are quick to chase away predators such as gulls. I hoped that this would be the ultimate gull deterrence plan. Alas, I was able to restore terns, but there was one problem with

Gulls are generalist predators that eat a wide range of foods. Some learn to hunt seabirds such as terns. Terns know that gulls are a threat and avoid islands where the gulls are nesting. Project Puffin Photo.

this plan. Gulls nest earlier than terns by several weeks and terns were reluctant to start new colonies too close to gulls.

Decoys worked so well to attract terns, I thought perhaps I could use human decoys to chase off gulls. Perhaps robots could eventually replace our human seabird keepers. I tried a few simple "scaregulls," but they had little effect. The most spectacular failure was Robo-Ranger.

In the spirit of cornfield scarecrows, David Buchner, a friend and middle-school science teacher at Dewitt Middle School in Ithaca, New York, had his class build a life-sized solar-powered robot. They purchased a used department store mannequin which the students called "Jack" because he lived in a box. I called the creation "Robo-Ranger" because I liked the ring of the name and thought if this was successful, we would set out a small army of the robots to help us keep gulls off of nesting islands.

I hoped the robot would look frightening because he held a fake rifle and popped out of his plywood box at random times. But between rain and salty sea spray, Robo-Ranger quickly rusted in an upright position. Gulls began landing and pooping on its head. They certainly had the last laugh. Once again, gulls taught me a lesson in humility. They easily distinguished the robot from our resident seabird stewards, even though they were dressed alike. Now I know that gulls can recognize

To test the idea that a robot could keep gulls away from nesting puffins and terns, we created Robo-Ranger in 2008 at the Dewitt Middle School in Ithaca, NY. The robot was put in place at Egg Rock and dressed to look like the resident researchers, such as Juliet Lamb—here dressed in a similar way to Robo-Ranger. However, gulls quickly learned that there was nothing to fear from the robot. Lesson learned: never underestimate the intelligence of birds. Photo by Stephen Kress.

individual researchers and stay just out of rifle range if they feel threatened.

I have not only come to realize that birds are surprisingly smart and adaptable, I also have great admiration for how they live in the fast lane of life, requiring abundant, high quality food and clean air. Just as caged canaries were once used to test air quality in mines, birds today are warning us of degraded and dangerous environmental conditions.

In the 20th century, disappearing eagles, ospreys, and peregrine falcons exposed the nightmare effects of DDT and helped to make a case for banning it in the United States. Today, seabirds suffer from the "agriculture" of the ocean as factory fishing scoops their preferred foods out of the depths. Four times as much forage fish (small fish eaten by ocean predators) is taken out of the oceans today as in the 1960s. Ninety percent of forage fish catch ends up at fish farms and as pig and poultry feed. The world's pigs and poultry now eat six times more fish than Americans!

Most of the Atlantic herring in the Gulf of Maine are captured and used as lobster bait, depriving puffins and other ocean predators from a key source of food. Photo by NOAA.

Many of our most beloved wildlife species, such as Bald Eagles, Ospreys, pelicans, gannets, gulls, and herons depend on forage fish such

Peregrines were lost from most of the United States as a casualty of the pesticide DDT. Because of much hard work from friends of the peregrine, such as falconers and wildlife professionals, they are back throughout their North American range. In some cases, they kill terns and puffins. Here, a Peregrine Falcon sits with its catch, a Common Tern. Resident island stewards record these events and chase the peregrines away from rare seabirds when they have an opportunity. Photo by Siyu Wang.

as menhaden and herring. Predatory fish such as salmon and even whales and seals also depend on them. But how long will the forage fish and all of the animals that depend on them last? That is up to generations after me to decide.

Even Roland Clement, one of my biggest defenders when critics questioned the usefulness of Project Puffin, once told Derrick (when Roland was a sharp 99 years old!), "Project Puffin was a stop-gap measure to provide for the possibility of a puffin comeback."

I think what Clement meant was that we can no longer be certain of whether an animal will exist at a fixed spot, but we can work hard to assure they will exist somewhere. The restoration of a puffin breeding colony at the edge of its range in Maine, my original goal, is no longer my end goal.

At a local level, I want puffins to grow to a number where they can adapt to the changes that people are imposing on them. I also hope our success with puffins inspires people to create and improve habitat for wildlife everywhere. Every species needs a champion. The opportunities are virtually unlimited.

For some species, habitat protection or enhancement will help. But where we once believed that putting aside land for national parks and stopping hunting of migratory birds would be enough to restore the balance of nature, we now know better. Humans have so tilted the odds that there is no such thing as balance.

When I narrate seabird cruises to Egg Rock, I have told the eager puffin watchers, "Every puffin we see is a miracle." Now I see that the miracle of puffins at Egg Rock would end without the dedicated wildlife stewards who live on this and other nesting islands to protect the birds and stand guard against predators, invasive plants, abandoned fishing gear and disruptive human visitors. The puffins and terns on Maine islands are examples of 'conservation reliant species' that depend on people for their survival.

Sarah Guitart and Nadia Swanson search for Roseate Tern nests at Eastern Egg Rock. Photo by Jean Hall.

New threats to wildlife continue to appear. As we write these pages, the novel coronovirus (COVID 19) pandemic threatens to keep the seabird stewards off the puffin islands this summer, due to stay-at-home orders. Without people living among the seabirds to protect them, much of the progress achieved over recent decades could erode. Only ongoing funding and protection for "conservation reliant" species will assure their survival in the face of new and existing threats.

In a similar way, it will take an ongoing small army of beach patrollers, marsh protectors and forest champions to make sure that these habitats and their wildlife survive. The negative impacts of people on the planet are increasingly easy to see. The long list of human-caused global threats, including habitat lost to development, pollution, climate change, and general loss of biodiversity, should serve as our call to action. It is foolish to expect nature to stay in balance despite our reckless ways. Even if we care only for our own health and that of our families, then we should pay attention to the birds, in order to save both them and ourselves.

Is it possible on our crowded coastlines to restore species and expect them to sustain their own numbers without our help? Is there a balance of nature? It is time for people to recognize that humans are causing most of the problems for life on Earth, and it is now time to accept a stewardship role. I no longer worry when people call this "playing God." As my Canadian colleague Tony Diamond put it, "It's time somebody played God after our predecessors played the devil for so long." Or as my early mentor Bill Drury said, "If we don't play God, the gulls will."

2019 Eastern Egg Rock team. Photo by Derrick Jackson.

12.
MAKING A
DIFFERENCE

When I started Project Puffin, I was 26, aided only by my research assistant, Kathy Blanchard. As our success on Eastern Egg Rock spread to other islands in Maine and around the world, I handed off most of the day-to-day wildlife management details to eager college students.

Today, more than 700 interns have spent summers on our Maine islands. Scores have gone on to fulfilling careers in state and federal wildlife agencies, zoos, conservation organizations and environmental groups. The work of "graduates" of Project Puffin stretches from Alaska to Antarctica, from the United Kingdom to the South Pacific and from Bermuda to China.

Their success and achievements give me pride. I never expected that our vision of returning puffins to Egg Rock would capture the imagination of so many inspiring young biologists. I know that our success at Egg Rock would not have been possible without their dedication and very hard work. Their stories serve as a model for what is possible when smart, determined people set out to change the world. Space does not allow me to tell all the stories, but a few will show how individuals are making a difference for wildlife.

Kathy Blanchard became a seabird conservation leader among isolated fishing communities along the north shore of the Gulf of St. Lawrence that hunted puffins as traditional food. By the 1970s, those traditions had slashed the puffin population in one region from 62,000 birds to 15,000. Kathy worked with those communities, demonstrating how caring children could influence family members to stop puffin hunting. By 1988, puffin numbers rebounded to 35,000.

After leaving Project Puffin, Tom French directed endangered species programs for the Commonwealth of Massachusetts. He said he had "the best job in the world," climbing into bald eagle nest trees and rappelling off cliffs, buildings and bridges to band peregrine falcon chicks. One of his final projects in this job was to reintroduce rattlesnakes to former habitat in Massachusetts. This idea likely sprouted directly from Project Puffin.

Kevin Bell left Project Puffin in 1975 to be the youngest curator ever at Chicago's Lincoln Park Zoo. Today he directs the entire zoo. He has led efforts to save the Bali Mynah, a bird that disappeared due to poaching on its only home on Bali Island, Indonesia. Today the Bali Mynah has a wild population again, thanks to reintroductions from zoos.

Another "Puffineer" of the 1970s and 80s, Richard Podolsky, became a consultant on protecting birds in the design and construction of wind turbines, power lines, and reflective glass in skyscrapers, including those in New York City's new World Trade Center complex. Building collisions kill 600 million birds each year in the United States, second only to the 1.4 billion carnage from outdoor cats. Richard once said, "There is nothing harder I will ever do than what we did on Egg Rock. Cutting and hauling mounds of sod to create our puffin nesting condos and landing in small boats in often extreme conditions. There were always risks getting in and out of boats

Grubbing for puffins at Egg Rock.
Photo by Derrick Jackson.

and plenty of bumps and scrapes." He said that in the fifteen years he helped collect puffin chicks in Newfoundland, he never took safety for granted. "Anyone could have fallen a hundred feet down those steep slopes onto the rocks. Disaster loomed around every corner collecting and taking care of the chicks. We were creative, with almost nothing."

There was one thing that was as mentally hard as the physical work. It is the killing of beautiful animals to save others.

Sue Schubel is one of Project Puffin's longest-serving staff, acting in many capacities over the years. When Sue first came to Project Puffin, she said "I never wanted to kill anything." That changed in 1988 when she was living on Eastern Egg Rock as field crew supervisor. She noticed that terns were hovering oddly, dipping down, then hovering again, but never landing. On closer inspection, she found 27 dead terns on their nests. Then she spotted a bold mink, a member of the weasel family.

Sue Schubel with a Murremaid Music Box sound system that plays seabird sounds and helps to start new colonies. She builds these systems and installs them worldwide. Photo by Stephen Kress.

This stunned her because it was the first four-legged mammal anyone had seen on Egg Rock in the fifteen years of the project. It had managed to swim at least two miles from the nearest island. Mink are well known bird killers, and this one had already left many terns dead. At that time there were only 16 pairs of puffins on

Egg Rock. Sue did everything she could to scare the mink off the island. She tried to bait it into live traps, but that didn't work. Eventually, she was able to shoot it. If she had not pulled the trigger, Project Puffin might have ended that summer.

The dilemma was no different in 2004, when Christina Donehower was an Egg Rock intern. Her protective eye for animals was honed as a child in Gig Harbor, Washington, where her pet ducks followed her into the water when she went kayaking. She was so attached to her ducks that she occasionally took them to school. "Growing up, I always played this caretaking role," she said. "I had to keep my eye on all of them, as there were foxes, raccoons, eagles, neighborhood dogs, and other predators in the area that posed a serious threat to the ducks."

Christina used that eye when a particular Herring Gull terrorized the Egg Rock tern colony for weeks. Christina and Egg Rock supervisor Ellen Peterson nicknamed it Split Tail for its missing tail feathers. "It would go into a colony, catch a tern fledgling, then a Great Black-backed Gull would steal that tern from the Herring Gull," Christina said. "Then Split Tail would go back in, get another tern chick and

Christina Donehower was fascinated by pet ducks when she was a child. Now her research focuses on seabirds such as this eider duck.
Photo by Stephen Kress.

the Great Black-backed Gull would steal that one too. This repeated over and over, but Split Tail was very wary of people. Just when I'd get my aim [with her rifle], it flew away."

Ellen Peterson, Christina's supervisor, said Split Tail was so elusive that it earned Christina's highest respect. "She loved that gull," Ellen said of Christina. "She kept saying how Split Tail was one of the most amazing predators she'd ever seen. It was by far the most notorious gull on the island. It was so agile that it actually stole a lot of chicks back from the black-backs. Christina would go on

Christina Donehower with a Great Black Black-backed Gull which she has marked for her Ph.D. research on the impact of gull predation on terns. Photo by Ellen Peterson.

the roof of the cabin with her scope from four o'clock in the morning until dark. Every day we had some discussion of Split Tail. Christina would come down for a break and have her breakfast tea and I would have coffee and she would tell me how many terns Split Tail had taken. All day long, she saw chicks gobbled up."

Finally, on August 1, 2004, Christina recorded this in our Egg Rock journal: "At 15:00, I saw Split Tail, a well-known predatory Herring Gull. This bird hunted daily in the tern colony in the early morning and late afternoon/evening. Split Tail was shot while he was in the process of consuming a banded Roseate Tern fledgling."

Roseate Terns are an endangered species. At the time Egg Rock supported the largest colony of the species in Maine. Christina made the hard choice to shoot an individual predator that she admired—in the hope that she could help an endangered species survive. She went on to receive her Ph.D. based on her detailed studies of gull and tern predation at Egg Rock and has made a career working with rare and endangered seabirds.

As often happens at Egg Rock, mentors are just a few years older than their students. In 2006, when Christina became Egg Rock supervisor, Juliet Lamb was another Egg Rock rookie who was troubled by the dilemma of gull control.

Juliet was a brilliant, shy girl from Cape Cod, who entered Harvard University with sophomore standing, graduating at age nineteen. She was an accomplished French horn musician and enjoyed serenading seabirds from the roof of the Egg Rock Hilton. She felt at peace among the seabirds, but she was disillusioned with the culture at Harvard. She felt everyone was looking over each other's shoulder in fear of being left out and left behind. "Crazy as it might sound, you got the sense that it's not that cool to be passionate about things."

Juliet Lamb rowing. Photo by Jennifer Knight.

Juliet had never shot a firearm before Project Puffin. When asked if she would be comfortable around the shooting of puffin predators, even if she herself did not pull the trigger, her head went spinning.

"I had to really think about that," Juliet said. "My senior thesis was why we should never have to shoot coyotes, even if they were eating tern eggs. I was thinking if you kill off coyotes, you have to look at all the ripple effects, and part of the problems we've created is because we're doing so many things as a society without thinking about ripple effects."

On one of her first days on Egg Rock, she spotted a badly crippled gull. Juliet said, "It seemed to look at me with its eyes saying, 'Do something. Help me.'" Juliet helped it by shooting it. "In some ways, that was easier than letting it suffer," she said. "But it was so hard." As it has for many young people, Juliet's Egg Rock experience has helped to define her life's direction. She went on to become a seabird researcher for the Royal Society for the Protection of Birds on Scotland's Orkney Island and completed her Ph.D. as a pelican researcher in South Carolina.

Over time, it hit me that even though this was more than a half-century removed from my childhood in suburban Ohio, the new interns came from virtually the same background as mine.

I cared about puffins in the 1970s because I first cared about skinks in the 1950s. All of the seabird stewards of Egg

Rock and other Project Puffin islands were here because they first cared about animals near their childhood homes.

There is also another common feature that brought them to Egg Rock. They had backgrounds where they were largely unplugged from electronics. This realization was crystallized for me in 2009 when Derrick and I were on the island for one of his annual puffin reports in the *Boston Globe*. Juliet was supervisor and greeted us at the Hilton with interns Yvan Satge and Liz Zinsser.

Yvan came to us from France on an international fellowship funded by Peggy and Dur Morton. Liz had just graduated from Hobart and William Smith in upstate New York. Derrick asked them what they remembered about their childhoods that helped them appreciate nature to the degree that they relished their isolated summer on Egg Rock. With almost no hesitation, Juliet said: "We didn't watch TV."

Yvan Satge counting birds at Eastern Egg Rock. Photo by Sandy Flint.

Yvan said: "We didn't have TV either."

Liz said: "We had TV but no video games."

It was not my original intent, but I now realize that Project Puffin is not only a refuge for puffins but also an outpost for young adults who, like me, were allowed as children to explore the outdoors without fear of getting muddy.

When Derrick asked Juliet, Yvan, and Liz why they were predisposed to loving nature, an outpouring of free-play memories flowed: cemetery hide and seek; feeding an orphaned baby bird with scrambled eggs; picking mushrooms with grandparents; playing in tree houses; making maps; catching lizards; chasing birds.

"When my mother got bored with us indoors," Liz said, "she gave us a salt shaker and sent us outside, saying if we sprinkled salt on a bird's tail, we would catch it. Of course, they always flew away. But it made me always want to hold a bird." Juliet said, "Watching wildlife is like an addiction, to see life in all that complexity. It's free, easy to see and available to you, depending on where your imagination takes you. I'd rather be here than anywhere else."

We've had daughters and sons of early Puffineers become interns themselves. The first was Kiah Walker, the daughter of Diane DeLuca, a Project Puffin assistant in 1981, the year the first puffin pairs nested.

Diane moved on from puffins to become a biologist for New Hampshire Audubon where she led a very successful project to restore tern colonies at remote islands using non-lethal approaches to manage gulls—like noise makers and dogs that spooked gulls off the restoration islands early in the nesting season. Kiah came to Project Puffin in 2012 when she was a 19-year-old sophomore at Williams College. She has since volunteered on albatross conservation projects for the Midway Atoll National Wildlife Refuge to the far northwest of Hawaii.

When she was on Egg Rock she said: "To be here now and to know my mom built the puffin burrows and the petrel burrows and saw the first ones come back to nest is amazing."

Eastern Egg Rock has become even more special as we understand how human-caused climate change is disrupting life on even remote islands. Unfortunately, our country does not have a plan to confront the climate crisis. After President Barack Obama ended his time in office by creating and expanding national marine monuments, the 2016 elections ushered in President Donald Trump.

President Trump handed over the Environmental Protection Agency, the Interior Department and the Agriculture Department to leaders from the fossil fuel and chemical industries. Those agencies in turn launched unprecedented cuts to science and stewardship programs and rollbacks of cornerstone regulations protecting air, land and water for Americans. He has also backed the United States away from international cooperation with those trying to control climate change.

These changes have made Project Puffin interns angry and even more dedicated than before. The Egg Rock supervisor for 2017 and 2018, Laura Brazier, took part in the March for Science in Washington, DC. Fellow 2017 intern Alyssa Eby, an environmental biology graduate of the

University of Manitoba, added, "If you can deny science, you can deny what needs to be done. A lot of people would rather find ways to skip the science and live in their world without thinking about the consequences."

Brazier added, "Sometimes I wonder what we're doing out here in the grand scheme of things. How can five people on this tiny island help save the planet? But then I remind myself that these amazing birds were not here when the project started. That's how I stay hopeful! People brought them back, and I am part of this miracle."

Eastern Egg Rock 2018 Crew. Photo by Derrick Jackson.

In her own wonderment, the supervisor of the 2019 crew, Sarah Guitart, a marine science graduate from Boston University, said "I don't know if we're doing much to fight climate change out here, but if the fish data proves useful, we will know that we played a small part."

I never cease to be impressed by how the next generation of puffineers care so much about their role as seabird stewards. In a 2018 feature Derrick did for The *American Prospect Magazine*, he quoted the anguish of the interns as puffins brought in useless butterfish for their chicks during a nearly disastrous heat wave.

"It was devastating when the switch to butter-fish occurred," said Nicole Faber, a graduate of Bow-doin College. "The worst is watching a tern chick trying to stretch its mouth, get the fish halfway down."

Sarah Guitart and Angel Mendez inspect the wing of a puffin chick at Egg Rock to determine its age.
Photo by Jean Hall.

Audrey Holstead, a graduate of Texas A&M, re-called another tern chick that kept rejecting a butterfish. Its parent kept picking it up over and over again to keep try-ing to feed it. She said: "I'm sitting in the blind mentally screaming to myself, 'Drop the stupid thing!' I wince every time I see it."

But it was also Holstead who was in her bird blind late in the 2018 season when she saw a puffin zoom onto Eastern Egg Rock with its beak stuffed with fish. It soon disappeared un-der the boulders into a burrow that the crew had not yet added to their annual tally. That

Healthy puffin chicks demonstrate healthy marine conditions. Here, Nadia Swanson pulls a puffin chick from its nest for measurement, while supervisor Sarah Guitart calls for the banding equipment and scales.
Photo by Jean Hall.

burrow turned out to be the 173rd burrow, breaking the previous record for the island. "I just wanted to jump up and
down and scream to the world," Holstead says. "I did a little
wiggly dance."

Now the birds are screaming to the world. Their message is to stop climate change, pollution, and overfishing
while there is still time. If we listen to the birds, future generations will celebrate our stewardship.

I find hope from the puffins and the hundreds of inspiring young people that I have met along the way. These
ever-positive biologists share my passion and dedication to
do what it takes to help wild animals live in wild places. My
vision of long ago to bring back the puffins convinces me
not to be discouraged by those who say "it will never work."
Worthy, new ideas usually need a big supply of persistence
and dedication.

*Charlie Governali banding
terns at Eastern Egg Rock.*
Photo by Bob Butaky.

I am also convinced that with
enough creativity, it is possible to
bring animals back to places where
people forced them to retreat. Helping them thrive in the long term
gives added reason for teamwork.
A guiding message is that success
follows when people use science
to make observations and shape
thoughtful, long-range conservation plans.

Puffins have shown me the power of good people working hard for wildlife. These successes become more convincing every year as wildlife heroes around the world demonstrate through their hard work and innova-

Mary Kathryn Devers, a member of the 2019 team releases a puffin after weighing and measuring. Photo by Jean Hall.

tion that it is possible to protect and restore rare animals. Yet these heroes cannot work alone. Everything is connected to everything else. That is why we can only save species when most people understand that their day-to-day actions make a difference. Thoughtless living will bring an end to countless species unless we protect oceans and lands and do everything possible to make sure that no species are lost along the way.

To save species will take many more caring people who see the connections between our lifestyles and the health of wildlife and people. We can all do much more. I hope those who read this book will find their own conservation projects, make changes to their own lifestyles and find ways to share their love for wildlife with others. Becoming part of the solution is much more fun than being part of the problem!

One person can make a huge difference; many people working together can save this living planet.

EPILOGUE
REVELATIONS FROM THE EGG ROCK BIRD BLIND

N ormally, to protect the birds, few people receive permission to land on Egg Rock during the nesting season.

But I've long felt that it is important to go an extra step with teens in the hope of impressing upon them what a conservation victory looks like. This is more important than ever, as today's teens will become tomorrow's wildlife stewards at a time when humans are affecting every corner of the planet. If we are to save species, then each generation must pass our precious wildlife of today onto the next generation. Because today's teens are the future stewards for protecting the increasing number of conservation reliant wildlife species, we invite participants in the Hog Island program called "Coastal Maine Bird Studies for Teens" to spend a day on Egg Rock.

I like to believe that teens who have a powerful experience in nature will continue down the conservation path. Hopefully, they will be more likely as adults to become active participants in the preservation—rather than the decimation—of species. That could involve assisting with bird counts and other community science activities, volunteering for river clean-ups and someday perhaps joining zoning boards for land preservation. Saving wildlife can also happen in the solitude of a voting booth, pulling the lever for politicians who value clean water and air.

There are many ways to help wildlife, but assuming that someone else is going to step forward will most certainly lead to further losses rather than recovery. The world needs more conservation heroes.

Following are the impressions of three of the Hog Island teens who visited Egg Rock in 2019. They represent the kind of young people who could become conservation heroes. They are curious, caring, and as excited about a puffin with fish as other people are about a victory by their favorite sports team. Seeing through their eyes, I have renewed hope that puffins and other wildlife are in good hands.

Isaiah Scott, 16, peered out from his bird blind on Eastern Egg Rock and saw the avian world as he had never seen it before. "You felt like you were one with the natural setting," he said. "You saw all these birds nesting two feet in front of you. The view

Isaiah Scott, 16, from greater Savannah, Georgia, said it was inspiring to be on Eastern Egg Rock, "where a bird was hunted and driven to extinction, and now it's thriving." Photo by Luke Franke.

was astonishing. The rocks. The pristine waters. It was the closest I've ever been to a bird.

"Before, it's kind of like I was separated from them by my binoculars. You can see beautiful birds with them, but there's still something between you and them."

The most beautiful sight, he said, was a puffin with about 20 fish in its mouth. It stopped for just a moment before going down into the burrow.

"I saw the fish glimmer in the sun," Isaiah said. "I thought to myself, 'How can it catch all those fish and transport them?'"

Janelle Booker, 18, had similar wonderment in her Eastern Egg Rock blind. "You always see puffins on TV documentaries," she said, "but when you see them in person, Wow! You see them for a split second bringing in fish, pop down, pop up, disappear and then the cycle starts again a few minutes later. The cycle of seeing them go in and out is something I can't compare to anything else.

Janelle Booker, 18, from greater Atlanta, said her time on Eastern Egg Rock makes her want to study avian disease transmission. While on Hog Island, she sketched the details of mounted seabirds.
Photo by Luke Franke.

"My friends call it a flying penguin. I've tried to make them understand that they are very different from penguins, but it doesn't really work."

Matthew Gilbert, 16, said his time in an Egg Rock blind was a dream come true. A Maine native, he had previously circled Eastern Egg Rock on summer puffin tours.

Although 16-year-old Matthew Gilbert, an avid birder from near Portland, ME, lives only about 70 miles from Egg Rock, he was wowed by his time in the Egg Rock blind. "It's a dream come true!"
Photo by Lisa Gilbert.

"On the boat trips, the tour guide talked about the interns on the island taking care of the puffins," he said. "I thought to myself,

'I wish I could be an intern,' but I never knew I would actually have a chance to be on the island."

When the chance came, Matthew could barely keep up with what he saw. "It was puffins and razorbills always flying by, streaming across the water," he said. "But then, a puffin with fish in its mouth came in and sat down on a rock only 15 feet away from me. I have a video of it. It was so amazing to be able to look at it like that."

Isaiah is a junior at South Effingham High School, a half hour northwest of Savannah, Georgia. Janelle is a senior at Norcross High School, 40 minutes northeast of Atlanta. Matthew is a sophomore at Greely High School, 11 miles north of Portland.

Isaiah said he had such an experience. He says he is now paying attention to local wildlife postings by the Georgia Department of Natural Resources. "It definitely inspired me to be at a place where a bird was hunted and driven to extinction, and now it's thriving and producing more and more chicks," he said.

"Today in our language and writing class we had to write an essay the relationship between humans and animals in the natural world. I wrote about how, since the dawn of humankind, we've reduced animal and plant species and interrupted the harmony for our conveniences. I wrote about how humans have challenged the natural world.

"I haven't finished it yet, but I'm going to also talk about birds, and how so many species were once very common and now extinct."

Janelle said that before going onto Egg Rock, she wanted to be a pet veterinarian. She said that she now wants to specialize in avian disease transmission. "I was speaking with one of the speakers at camp who works with tufted puffins," she said. "I told him that I wanted to be a veterinarian and he said, "We can use those in Alaska, because there's a lot of diseases."

Matthew said that his love of birdwatching, which began at a very early age when his mother enrolled him in local Audubon summer camps, is now on steroids. In 2019, he recorded the second-highest number of bird species in the state of Maine for a teenager—220. He picked up 65 species on a Boy Scout canoe trip up the Allagash River. He spotted 64 species on a fall warbler migration extravaganza on an island in Casco Bay.

"There were 5,000 warblers in two hours," Matthew said. There's a bridge out onto the island. In all the shrubs below, there were so many warblers everywhere."

Matthew has also interviewed me for a documentary on Project Puffin and how our techniques are being used around the world. He entered his video into the National History Day competition. As of this writing, his work has made it out of the regionals for state judging.

"To see the influence of Project Puffin," Matthew said, "It's almost like saving the Ivory-Billed Woodpecker."

I am excited about these young people for other reasons. Matthew, who says he wants to go on to study large ecosystems, is a teen who has prioritized the outdoors over electronics. In the year 2020, he does not own a cell phone. He had one but he ran it over with a snowblower. After it was fixed, it was destroyed in a puddle on a camping trip. "My parents offered me another one, but I decided against it," Matthew said. "I found I was wasting more time on it than doing good things with it. It's not as hard as one might think to go without one."

Isaiah and Janelle are African American. Conservation leadership is going to have to be far more diverse if the movement is to have a future in a nation where people of color will become the majority by mid-century.

Given the current whiteness of most major conservation groups, and media coverage of white icons of concern for climate change, from former Vice President Al Gore to Swedish teen Greta Thunberg, it might surprise some people to know that people of color are far more likely than white Americans to say in polls that climate change is a very serious problem.

Much of that is due to the nation's environmental racism, saddling communities of color with fossil fuel facilities and fossil fuel exhaust from highways. People of color are more likely to live in urban heat islands that will become more fatal with global warming and less likely to be able to recover from the damage of hurricanes, which are becoming more intense.

Right now, Isaiah is a teenager reveling at the sight of painted buntings, swallow-tailed kites, and red-cockaded woodpeckers. He hopes for the day when he no longer sticks out in a crowd of birders and when no one asks him in surprise, "How did YOU get involved?" He says, "When I get that question, I'm thinking, "Am I not supposed to get into this? Am I supposed to play basketball or be in a gang?' It's not a bad thing to be different. I hope I'm part of inspiring others to realize it's OK to be part of this and express themselves."

Janelle is similarly proud of her world of looking for hawks, egrets, grackles and hummingbirds. She hopes that more teens will look like her, carrying a pair of binoculars. She said birdwatching is a metaphor for life. "I've learned that the absence of evidence is not the evidence of absence," she said. "So many times, I'll look for birds and not see them, but when I pay closer attention, I find them. It's taught me not to be so quick to give up on something."

Funny, that's exactly what I had to learn nearly a half century ago when I started Project Puffin. Many people thought I should give up after eight years of waiting to see a puffin bringing fish home to its chick.

It does my heart good to close this book by knowing that young people like Janelle, Isaiah and Matthew are filled with the spirit to pay attention to birds, helping the world to see what it previously could not.

Make an author happy today! If you enjoyed this book, please consider posting an Amazon review. Even if it's only a few sentences, it would be a huge help.... and thank you!
                                        — *Stephen W. Kress, Derrick Z. Jackson*

Take Action for Seabirds

Because we are connected to everything else, small actions really help.
Together, we can make a big difference for seabirds!

Take action at home.

- Become educated about climate change: The Intergovernmental Panel on Climate Change's recent report (https://www.ipcc.ch/sr15/) says reducing carbon emissions is necessary to keep us below a safe level of warming (1.5°C). A carbon tax can help us transition from fossil fuels to clean, renewable energy sources

- Talk to your family, friends, and neighbors about why you care about seabirds and climate change.

- Encourage your family to consider energy efficiency when purchasing vehicles and household appliances such as refrigerators and freezers.

- Turn down air conditioning and heat.

- Turn off lights when leaving a room.

- Conserve water by not letting the tap run and taking shorter showers.

Reduce and recycle plastic -- most of it eventually reaches the oceans.

- Never release helium-filled party balloons (especially metallic ones). Too often they end up at sea where they can choke seabirds, marine mammals, and sea turtles.

- Avoid using single-use plastics, including straws, utensils, and bags. Bring your own bags and containers. Explain your reasons to restaurant and supermarket staff.

- Pick up and recycle plastics along roadsides, sidewalks, and parks.

- Eat sustainable seafood.

- Before buying seafood at restaurants and supermarkets, check the Monterey Bay Aquarium's Seafood Watch program: https://www.seafoodwatch.org/ Download the app.

- At restaurants, ask your server if their seafood comes from sustainablesources.

- Look for the Marine Stewardship Council logo on seafood packaging. https://www.msc.org/home

Create bird-friendly habitats at home and in schoolyards.

- Avoid fertilizers and yard pesticides. These can poison backyard wildlife and runoff your land, eventually reaching lakes and oceans.

- Replace lawns with plantings that provide more food and cover for wildlife. Less lawn mowing also reduces air pollution.

- Plant native plants to provide food for birds and other wildlife.

- Provide nest boxes and brush piles for shelter

Encourage the adults in your life to vote for representatives that care about ocean conservation and climate change.

Join groups that advocate for birds and climate change policy such as the National Audubon Society www.audubon.org and 350.org (www.350.org).

Support seabird conservation by "adopting" a puffin. http://projectpuffin.audubon.org

ACKNOWLEDGMENTS

My deepest thanks go to the more than 700 "puffineers"—the young biologists that live with the seabirds on Maine Islands. Their great commitment has made every step of Project Puffin possible. I thank David Nettleship and the Canadian Wildlife Service for their collaboration and thank the staffs of the Maine Coastal Islands NWR and Maine Dept. of Inland Fisheries and Wildlife for their ongoing support. I also thank my co-author Derrick Jackson for the research, interviews and writing that he contributed to this book and thank our publisher, Penny Noyce for guiding *The Puffin Plan's* journey from vision to print. The book benefitted greatly from designer Yu-Yi Ling who merged our story with dynamic photographs donated by so many talented photographers. I am especially pleased to share the amazing travels of an Atlantic Puffin, Manx Shearwater and Arctic Terns with maps that reveal for the first time their remarkable journeys. For these, I thank Annette Fayet, Mark Baren, Linda Welch and Michael Langlois for creating seabird tracking maps. The chapter 'The Case of the Missing Fish' greatly benefited from the review of oceanographer, Dr. Lewis S. Incze. I also thank my wife, Elissa Wolfson and daughter Liliana Pearl Kress for reading the text and offering helpful suggestions. I look forward to more island adventures with my son Nathan and grandson Max. Their enthusiasm gives me hope for the puffin's future. — S.K.

My loving thanks go to my wife Michelle Holmes, for prodding Steve and I with hard questions to focus us on the purpose of our Project Puffin writings and to her and my youngest son Tano and his wife Clarissa for their suggestions to assure diverse voices of the next generation in this book. I of course also thank Steve for inviting me into the inner "burrows" of Project Puffin. And I owe a great debt of gratitude to my late mentor and editor, Les Payne of Newsday. He understood ahead of his time that it was important for people of color to cover environmental issues and sent me to the Eastern Egg Rock burrows for my first story on the project in 1986. Finally, I would like to thank my oldest son Omar, who as a child asked us to pick up a wounded blue jay by a biking trail in Wisconsin and cycle to a vet. I hope that is a metaphor for how the next generation will take care of a wounded planet. — D.Z.J.

ABOUT THE AUTHORS

STEPHEN W. KRESS is a world-renowned ornithologist. He is the founder of Project Puffin and retired Vice President of Bird Conservation for the National Audubon Society. He is a Visiting Fellow of the Cornell Laboratory of Ornithology.

Steve Kress with puffin chick.
Photo by Derrick Z Jackson

Derrick Jackson at Eastern Egg Rock in 2015 with a puffin fledger.

DERRICK Z. JACKSON is an award-winning former columnist for the Boston Globe. An accomplished photographer, his column was a finalist for the Pulitzer prize, and his UCS blog won a 2018 first prize from the National Society of Newspaper Columnists.